Remaking the Movies

DIGITAL CONTENT AND THE EVOLUTION OF THE FILM AND VIDEO INDUSTRIES

OECD

ORGANISATION FOR ECONOMIC CO-OPERATION AND DEVELOPMENT

The OECD is a unique forum where the governments of 30 democracies work together to address the economic, social and environmental challenges of globalisation. The OECD is also at the forefront of efforts to understand and to help governments respond to new developments and concerns, such as corporate governance, the information economy and the challenges of an ageing population. The Organisation provides a setting where governments can compare policy experiences, seek answers to common problems, identify good practice and work to co-ordinate domestic and international policies.

The OECD member countries are: Australia, Austria, Belgium, Canada, the Czech Republic, Denmark, Finland, France, Germany, Greece, Hungary, Iceland, Ireland, Italy, Japan, Korea, Luxembourg, Mexico, the Netherlands, New Zealand, Norway, Poland, Portugal, the Slovak Republic, Spain, Sweden, Switzerland, Turkey, the United Kingdom and the United States. The Commission of the European Communities takes part in the work of the OECD.

OECD Publishing disseminates widely the results of the Organisation's statistics gathering and research on economic, social and environmental issues, as well as the conventions, guidelines and standards agreed by its members.

Foreword

This report was presented to the Working Party on the Information Economy in December 2006 and May 2007 as part of its work on digital broadband content. It was recommended to be made public by the Committee for Information, Computer and Communications Policy in October 2007. Information in this report is current as at September 2007 but business changes in the industry occur frequently.

The report was prepared by Richard Hawkins, University of Calgary and Graham Vickery, OECD Secretariat, with the assistance of Kiranpal Sidhu and Ben Li, University of Calgary. The report is part of the work on digital broadband content under the direction of Graham Vickery, OECD Secretariat.

Table of Contents

SUMMARY

This study explores the implications of the creation, distribution and use of digital content on the structure, value chain and business models of the film and video industry, focusing mainly on implications for production and distribution of cinematic films and television programs. Key points emerging from the study include:

Product characteristics and markets

- The OECD area is the source of most of the value produced by the film and video industry. Although film and video markets in countries such as India and China are very large, their investments and revenues are still a very small fraction of the world total. Most of the total value (up to 80%) is produced in only a few OECD countries, led by English-language productions.

- During the past ten years, the number of cinema films produced per year in most major OECD markets has shown no substantial prolonged increase although there have been significant fluctuations in US production from year to year. In contrast, there has been a marked increase in the number of cinema screens and in the amount of post-release activity, mainly DVDs and television-based distribution. In particular, the number of titles available on DVD has surpassed the number of titles that were available on video cassettes by a considerable margin.

- Relative to all other media products, cinema and television entertainment requires by far the highest amount of initial investment per unit, most of which is high risk. Investors often adopt a venture capital model, financing a portfolio of productions, of which only a few are expected to be successful. In the feature film segment, average costs have soared over the past 20 years, driven largely by the 'blockbuster' phenomenon, where a large share of capital is invested in a small number of productions. Average costs have risen across the board, but much of the increase is in advertising and distribution, which now account for 30-40% of total costs for major studios.

- The economic viability of the industry depends upon average rates of return from a constantly diversifying portfolio of media and associated enterprises. This average can be maintained only where there is sufficient variety and volume of output, but also where the rate of production matches demand.
- The market success of film and video products is closely tied to consumer perceptions of quality, which is reflected in constantly escalating production values. Products are not price-sensitive, and price discounts tend not to encourage greater consumption of items with lower production values.
- Technology and market distinctions between cinema and television markets are breaking down. Most film and video products now depend on a wide spectrum of interrelated distribution channels, all of which are digitised or are increasingly becoming digitised into a set of related markets:
  - Cinema box office markets.
  - Television markets (incorporating cable, satellite and broadcast segments).
  - Consumer markets (including home video sales and rentals).
  - Online markets (including video services, interactive television, and wireless digital content).
- Consumption of audio-visual media and content tends to be cumulative rather than substitutive. New media such as DVDs and home entertainment centres tend to supplement and reinforce cinema and television consumption. Consumers who attend the most cinema performances also tend to buy more DVDs and watch more television. DVD and television release (mostly pay-TV and VoD) have become major profit sources, DVDs often earning 50% or more of total income.
- To this point in time, the online video download market has not developed as quickly or as comprehensively as many had expected. Compared to DVDs and television, downloading is not yet a substantial revenue stream for most film and video products. Television (including broadcast, pay-TV and VoD) is now overwhelmingly the most competitive distribution media for all types of film and video products, followed by DVD rentals and sales.
- Much digital film and video content is distributed by e-commerce, selling or renting DVDs online.

- Although existing legal download sites appear to be slow in achieving a substantial market share, 'social networks' show many signs of developing the consumer communities necessary to stimulate the online download market. Furthermore, these social networks also promise to change the paradigm of online distribution from basically a linear distribution process to a highly interactive environment.

Industry structure

- The markets for media products in the OECD countries overall is characterised by large, vertically integrated multinational conglomerates that own or have substantial interests in a wide range of audio, visual and print media as well as in communication networks of various kinds. A substantial portion of the Hollywood production cluster is now owned by conglomerates and investors that are not based in the US.
- For most of the largest of these groups, film and video entertainment products make up only about 25% of the product portfolio, and these businesses have invested particularly heavily in networking activities ranging from cable television networks to ISPs, portals and telecommunication undertakings, and increasingly in Internet-based businesses.
- The film and video investment and production structure is now distributed internationally. International contract and co-production initiatives have increased the value of domestic film and video output dramatically in several countries, most notably the UK, Canada and New Zealand.

The value chain

- The film and video value chain is already heavily digitised and dependent on high-speed Internet facilities. Most of the major production and post-production functions are computer-dependent. The production of music, sound and special effects is almost entirely digital as is most of the animation process. Remaining areas for digitisation are image capture in the cinema film segment and in parts of the television feature segment along with distribution in the cinema segment.
- The film and video value chain is highly complex because film and video entertainment products are intermediate goods. Once a film or video has been produced, various stakeholders invest and add value to it in various secondary and tertiary markets. Some of this is related to exhibition and distribution, but others exploit various spin-offs ranging from merchandising and advertising to the commercialisation of new technology.

- The technology of film and video production and distribution has changed substantively in the past 50 years but the basic value-added structure of the industry has remained intact. Although many digitised segments are now very mature, they have not caused major alteration in the basic value-added structure. However, significant challenges to this structure are likely from the elimination of remaining analogue bottle-necks, mostly concerning new digital image capture and digital distribution, with digital cinema technologies likely to be extremely significant.
- Full digitisation of production and post-production may have major effects on the value chain:
  - Greater integration of the production and post-production segments.
  - Redefinition and possible relocation of the duplication function.
  - Redefinition of the distribution function.
  - Closer integration of the cinema and television environments.
  - Creation of a new 'communication' value-added segment geared to exploiting new methods of interactive market research encompassing social networks.
- The cinema exhibition segment will eventually be converted to fully digitised production and distribution. The added flexibility of digital cinema may expand the range of products that are shown and enable market development that goes well beyond the exhibition of conventional feature films.
- Although digitisation of production and distribution has many cost advantages, the digital environment will not necessarily lower overall costs. In particular, film and video production will remain a human resource-intensive enterprise, and increasing skill and productivity levels may result in overall higher labour costs.
- Digitisation provides opportunities for more undertakings in more countries to add value to the film and video industries, *i.e.* by exploiting emerging specialist technology markets, without necessarily boosting domestic production of film products as such.

The policy framework

- Policies that impact the industry now include general innovation and technology policies, including R&D incentives and related human resource development initiatives, as the industry becomes increasingly digitised and software-intensive. Policies regarding competition, cultural issues, broadband infrastructure, industry promotion, production subsidies and IPR also remain important.
- Overall, the line between film and video policy and general 'information economy' or 'information society' policies has become blurred, in large measure due to governments promoting information technologies and the Internet as engines of economic growth. The new challenge for governments is to devise approaches to balance these evolving agendas in the public interest. In many cases this may not require the implementation of entirely new types of policies or policy-driven industry initiatives, but rather the shaping and redirection of existing policy to reflect new realities. In other cases, established policy approaches and attitudes may become less relevant, particularly taking into account the global nature of creation, production, distribution and use of film and video products.

Chapter 1

INTRODUCTION

Aims of this study

This study explores the implications of digital content for the structure, value chain and business models of the film and video industry. Film and video products can take a huge variety of forms from modest audio-visuals used in training or promotional contexts, to blockbuster feature films that cost and earn very large amounts of money in worldwide distribution. Production and distribution for any film or video product can involve an extremely wide array of commercial interests, sometimes with quite different strategies for the digitisation of film and video content.

The main focus of this study is commercial entertainment products, mainly regarding the production and distribution of cinematic films and television programs. The study analyses the impact of digital content creation, distribution and use on value chains and business models and explores the policy implications of these changes. Following the general approach developed in previous OECD studies on scientific publishing (OECD 2005a), music (OECD 2005b) and online computer and video games (OECD 2005c), the aim is to identify how digital content may affect the function and position of different participants in the industry value chain.

The study begins by defining the industry and outlining its economic significance and challenges. Analysis is then provided of key production and market trends (Chapter 2) and of the evolving structure of the industry (Chapter 3). This is followed by detailed analysis of the value chain (Chapter 4), likely changes to the value chain brought about by digitisation and technical change (Chapter 5), and the possible implications of these changes (Chapter 6). The report concludes with a discussion of the policy framework for this industry in the OECD countries and how it may evolve (Chapter 7).

Economic significance of the film and video industries

The production and distribution of films and videos is a significant industry in the OECD countries, although most of the high-volume commercial entertainment segment is situated in only a few countries – mainly the United States, Japan, Britain, France, Italy, Germany and Spain. Countries like Canada and Australia are significant producers and exporters of film and video entertainment products, but in effect they are part of a larger international bloc of English-language film and video producers. Smaller countries like Sweden and Denmark also have notable domestic film and video industries that are often successful in export markets, but their total output is very small.

There are no comprehensive data on the size of the film and video industries worldwide. However, the most recent available statistics for the US, which hosts the largest single part of the worldwide industry, gives an impression of the overall economic significance of this industry. In 2002, US-based motion picture undertakings comprising all commercial television and film market segments earned combined receipts from production, exhibition and associated activities (excluding film and video equipment manufacture) of over USD 62 billion, with over 19 000 motion picture industry establishments paying out just over USD 10.2 billion in wages and professional fees (US Business Census 2002). Between 2000 and 2005, on average 350 000 people were employed directly by the US motion picture industry.[1] This compares with the value of shipments from US auto manufacturers in 2002 of just under USD 98 billion, and computer hardware shipments of just under USD 47 billion.[2] Adding an estimate of similar receipts for non-US producers, receipts in the film and video industries worldwide are probably around USD 120-150 billion. Most of this is earned within the OECD region itself (which represents the single highest-value marketplace for film and video products) or otherwise involves film and video products exported from OECD countries.

1. Derived from US Bureau of Labor Statistics, National Industry-Specific Occupational Employment and Wage Estimates, NAICS 512100 - Motion Picture and Video Industries, 2000 to 2005.

2. Data are taken from the US Business Census industry series for manufacturing industries in 2002. The US Business Census does not produce a fully comparable value of shipment estimate for the motion picture industry.

Defining film and video industries

This particular study focuses upon audio-visual representations that are intended for public exhibition on a commercial basis, whether in cinemas, on television or in home entertainment formats (principally via video cassettes, DVDs or Internet downloads). The study is concerned mainly with cinema films and television entertainment programming (excluding live broadcasts). Enterprises involved in the manufacture of production and exhibition equipment, construction of exhibition facilities or consumer electronics manufacture have been excluded from the industry definition, although they are discussed where appropriate.

The full NAICS nomenclature for the film and video industry (NAICS Code 5121, see Appendix A) also includes commercial advertisements and music videos but these have largely been excluded from this particular study because they are associated mainly with the value chains of the advertising industry and the music industry respectively. Concerning television, the focus is on 'stock' programming (filmed dramatic, comedic and documentary programming), rather than 'flow' programming (mainly live broadcasts such as newscasts and sporting events). Live sporting events likewise can be considered as value chain segments in the sports industries. This narrowed definition is appropriate to the aims of the study because:

- Commercial entertainment represents a very high proportion of film and video production overall, encompassing all of the product group segments identified in the NAICS nomenclature.
- In terms of the challenges and opportunities for developing digital content markets, most of the current industry and policy issues centre on entertainment-related products.
- Producers of commercial, filmed entertainment products are major users of leading-edge technologies and often are major contributors to key areas of technological development and standards.

The study is concerned mainly with film and video production in the OECD countries, but the study also looks at the growth of this industry in significant emerging markets like India and China. If measured by production volume, currently India has the world's largest film industry, producing nearly twice as many feature films as the US each year (see Appendix B). The study does not cover the adult film industry, even though probably this segment is currently a more significant supplier of online content than any other single part of the film and video industries.

Industry characteristics

Most of the value added in film and video production comes from services related to production and exhibition. Of all the product groups listed under NAICS Code 5121 (motion picture and video industries), only the processing and duplication of films, DVDs or video cassettes represents a 'manufacturing' type of activity, and this generated only 1-2% of 2002 US industry receipts.[3] Overall the industry is mostly human resource-intensive. There is high investment in very specific skills or in some cases the personalities of individuals, and there can be extremely low substitutability of workers within any given skills segment. But many individual service segments are also capital-intensive – for example, studio, duplication and exhibition facilities, or highly specialised post-production and special effects laboratories.

Relative to all other media products, film and video productions require by far the highest amount of up-front investment, most of which is high risk. This is true especially at the top end – feature films and major network television programming. An independently made film with a very modest budget (under USD 1 million) occasionally may yield returns of several hundred percent, but in 2005, the Motion Picture Association of America (MPAA) reported that the average cost of a feature film from a major US studio (including duplicating, advertising and distribution) was over USD 96 million, and that the average costs for productions from affiliates of the major studios was just under USD 39 million (MPAA 2005a).[4] To put this in perspective, the average cost of a major studio production in 1985 was only about USD 23 million, indicating that there has been more than a four-fold average cost increase in just 20 years (MPAA 2005a).

These escalations in average costs doubtlessly reflect the 'blockbuster' effect, whereby in each yearly release cycle each studio produces a handful of very expensive productions. Typical recent costs associated with these films have been in the USD 300-500 million range, with occasional productions approaching the USD 1 billion mark (*Titanic* being the most expensive single film to date). Most Hollywood films cost substantially less

3. This estimate is based on the 2002 US Business Census figures for Motion Picture sector receipts. The classifications are not always clear as to which 'duplication' activities include related services as well as actual manufacturing of film negatives and prints, or of CDs, DVDs and videocassettes.

4. The MPAA is the main trade association of the Hollywood studios. Six major studio groups are 'full' MPAA members – Buena Vista Pictures and Distribution, Paramount Pictures Corporation, Sony Pictures Entertainment Inc., Twentieth Century Fox Film Corporation, Universal City Studios LLLP, and Warner Bros. Entertainment Inc. – whereas their directly owned subsidiaries are 'affiliated' members.

to produce, but sometimes may entail promotion and advertising costs similar to those of larger-budget productions (see Chapters 2 and 4). The average costs of a film produced entirely in the European Union are substantially less – between USD 6-7 million – but markets are substantially smaller. According to the European Audiovisual Observatory, films released in 2005 that were produced solely by European studios accounted for only about 30% of the European exhibition market (EAO 2005).

But in order to fully understand the dynamics driving escalations like these, it is essential to understand that the total cost of a film production is actually combination of two investment streams:

- *'Negative' costs* – related to producing the final film negative (including production costs, studio costs and capitalised interest).[5]
- *Print & advertising (P&A) costs* – incurred in duplicating, distributing, publicising and generally developing the market for the film.[6]

Once these streams are combined, the total is referred to as the 'theatrical cost' – *i.e.* the whole cost of making, marketing and distributing the film. In recent years a much greater proportion of the average cost increase has been attributable to P&A costs. In 1985, 'negative' costs (costs excluding print and advertising costs) represented on average about 72% of theatrical costs, but by 2005, as total costs rose sharply, P&A costs rose even more sharply and negative costs declined to 62% of the total. In other words, in addition to the four-fold increase in overall average costs between 1985 and 2005, the proportion of P&A costs increased by 10 percentage points (MPAA 2005a). For the major Hollywood studios these proportions appear to have settled over the past five-year period at an average of roughly 60% negative costs and 40% P&A costs. The situation with the affiliate studios is only slightly different – on average closer to 70% negative costs and 30% P&A costs.

More interesting in terms of the digitisation of various production and distribution processes is the split within the P&A stream itself between print and advertising costs. MPAA figures for 1955 and 1985 indicate that print costs as a whole have been declining, at least for the major studios. In 1955 they represented about 20% of P&A costs, declining to about 13% in 1995 and stabilizing thereafter. As a portion of total theatrical costs, between

5. The term 'negative' is used throughout this analysis for costs directly related to production of the final film negative.

6. P&A costs do not include cinema or television exhibition costs, borne by the exhibitor. They typically also do not include DVD production, which even if handled by the production company is considered to be an additional merchandising undertaking – not included in the production cost stream for the film as such.

1985 and 2005 it would appear that print costs have remained steady at approximately an average of 4% of the total. Thus, possible future savings from developments like digital cinema (see Chapter 5) appear to be somewhat offset by the general P&A increase which is due primarily to a higher advertising spend.

The advertising and promotion portion of P&A costs includes print media, billboards, radio and television, cinema trailers and the Internet. For both majors and affiliates in the US, the majority of the advertising spend was concentrated in print and broadcast media (about 70-75% on average) and also in various marketing and promotion-related services (about 20% on average). The Internet does not appear to be a major cost factor in the advertising mix, but considering the reportedly high visitor rates to motion picture-related websites, this now may well be a very cost-effective advertising medium. The advertising and promotion strategy of the industry overall would appear to remain based upon blanket coverage of all media outlets.

Technology and market domains

Historically, the film and video industries have been highly innovative and technological advances have long been recognised as an important way to enhance the commercial value of products. Production facilities in a typical television or film studio represent more than a century of continuous evolution in optics, lighting, sound recording, video display and special effects technologies. Much of the production process for both film and video is now computer-intensive. Although most cinema features are still distributed on analogue film, the content can be converted between analogue and digital formats at various points in the post-production process, with film editing, for example, almost always performed in a digital environment. Most special effects are partly or entirely computer-generated.

The primary historical distinction between film and video was that film was aimed originally at public exhibition on cinema screens whereas video was oriented entirely towards private consumption on a television screen. Essentially, a computer screen is a video application according to this distinction. In terms of business models, however, cinema films were marketed in the first instance to consumers, whereas television programs were marketed to advertisers. Basically, the business of television broadcasters was to deliver audiences to advertisers (Deband and Chetrit 2001; Caves 2000). With the advent of pay-TV, video on demand and 'sell-through' via video cassette and DVD, these historical distinctions have become blurred and there is now substantial crossover between film and video business segments with film products transposed to video media on a very large scale. However, the preferred production medium for many television programs (excepting news gathering, some serial programs and live broadcasts) is still cinematic film, although this is rapidly giving way to higher-definition digital imaging technologies (see Chapter 5). Otherwise, the production routine for a typical television program is little different from that of a cinema film.

The digitisation of audio-visual content presents many new business opportunities and challenges. For example:

- Digitally produced images are now of much higher quality than those produced by analogue video recorders, thus stimulating advances in exhibition technologies, particularly those aimed at home entertainment markets.
- Digital formats permit much more flexibility in how moving images can be produced, manipulated and distributed. This creates new production environments and special effects possibilities. But it also raises special problems for product security and integrity. Digitisation presents many legal and illegal 'image mining' possibilities and piracy is a major issue.
- Digital images can be distributed efficiently over broadband networks, both as direct online sales to individual consumers and as feeds to commercial exhibitors. This may increase pressures to decrease or even eliminate the time gap between cinema and online release dates. Digital distribution to cinemas also may reduce costs for producers.
- The digitised moving image may severely or entirely weaken the pre-determined temporal dimension of markets based upon film, video cassette or even DVD media, leading to a more prevalent 'multicast' environment for many products. In home entertainment markets, online distribution of digital audio-visual content allows consumers to choose when and where to view products. This has immediate implications for most current 'unicast' broadcast TV models (cable or terrestrial) which offer choice of channel but not choice of viewing time.

Underpinning all of these developments is the prospect of 'digital cinema', in which extremely fast photo sensors produce an image with most of the qualities of film (some of the technical issues and challenges are discussed in Chapter 5). If such technology succeeds in reducing production costs, it could make smaller independent producers more competitive, but also boost the efficiency of major studios. All of these issues are discussed further in Chapter 6.

Current challenges

The film and video industry faces escalating capital and production costs, profound technological change, and rapidly evolving consumer preferences and behaviours. Most of the challenges stem from the increasing number of consumer options as to how and when to consume film and video products.

Technological evolution and consumer behaviour

Digitised content is the latest stage in a series of technologically enabled changes in how consumers consume film and video products. These changes have affected primarily the temporal and spatial relationships between the picture and its viewers. They have occurred in several phases:

- The *theatrical* phase (from the invention of moving picture photography to *ca.* 1950): The viewer comes to the film. Viewing a moving picture of any type required that the viewer be in physical proximity to a projected film for a specified period of time.
- The *broadcast* phase (from *ca.* 1950 onward[7]): The film comes to the viewer. One showing of a film could be distributed simultaneously to many viewers in many locations via television. The viewer maintains physical proximity to the media but not to the picture. The viewer continues to consume within a specified time period.
- The *time-shift* phase (from *ca.* 1975 onward): The viewer controls the spatial and temporal relationships to the film. Home video recording devices removed the requirement that the film be consumed in a time period determined by the producer or the broadcaster. Moreover, a home recording could be used sequentially by different consumers at different points in time.
- The *archive* phase (from *ca.* 1975 onward): The video-rental model turned film archives into products for direct consumption. In addition to controlling the spatial and temporal relationships, the viewer determines which film will be viewed as well as when and where it will be viewed. Video rentals allowed the viewer to make a choice from thousands of cinema and television titles independently of any release or broadcast schedule.

7. Television pre-dates the 1950s, but the phase referred to here began with widespread proliferation of television network programming models that began in the late 1940s and early 1950s.

- The *sell-through* phase (from *ca.* 1980 onward): Archived films become available on cassette or DVD for outright sale to consumers. This phase placed the film industry in roughly the same commercial model as the publishing and music industries.
- The *video-on-demand* phase (*ca.* 1995 onward): Advances in broadband cable and online distribution remove the need to transfer film and video products to consumers in physical formats (DVDs or cassettes). Coupled with home recording this model eliminated the need to physically intermediate the direct acquisition of film products by consumers.
- The *home cinema* phase (from *ca.* 1995 onwards): Advances in video display technology (home entertainment centres) began to replicate the cinema experience more closely. Giant home video screens and high-fidelity sound systems brought the cinema experience into the home.

Significantly, each phase introduced new technologies and broadened the range of consumption alternatives while *not eliminating earlier models of consumption*. However, each additional new media has had substantial effects on existing media, typically resulting in audience reduction for the older media.

The box office as a barometer of changing consumption patterns

Cinema attendance is still key to many of these markets. MPAA figures indicate that with fluctuations in the 5% range, revenues from cinema exhibition in the US between 2000 and 2005 have averaged about USD 9 billion per year (MPAA 2005a). Table 1.1 shows US admission trends from 1985 to2005, which indicate that in all but five of these years, US box office receipts increased, growing by about 140% over the entire period.

It is significant that the time period in Table 1.1 exactly parallels the period of greatest change in both technology and consumption patterns for the film and video industry as a whole. But although changes in box office revenues fluctuated there is no clear link between the emergence of a new technology (like the videocassette or pay-TV) and box office revenues. Rises of around 13% in 1989 and 2002 are followed by declines in the following years. Overall, relative receipt stability never persists for periods of more than four consecutive years (1996-99 being the most stable period).

Likewise, during the period of greatest change in the technological and commercial environment (*i.e.* 1990-2002), cinema revenues grew steadily. The first significant overall decline in the 1985-2005 period occurs after 2002 where for the first time box office figures appear to establish a downward trend. However, it is not clear if this recent fall-off in receipts is due to new circumstances or to a departure from an otherwise continuing upward trend. The fluctuations show no obviously consistent relation to changing technological or market environments, and consumption and revenue fluctuations are not unusual for high-risk industries whose products encounter highly subjective evaluation by consumers. The important factor for the viability of these industries is sustaining overall upward growth, interspersed with highly profitable spikes in revenue.

Table 1.1. US box office growth, 1985-2005

Year	Box office gross (USD millions)	% change	
		Previous period	Compared with 2005
2005	8 991.2	-5.7	---
2004	9 539.2	0.5	-5.7
2003	9 488.5	-0.3	-5.2
2002	9 519.6	13.2	-5.6
2001	8 412.5	9.8	6.9
2000	7 660.7	2.9	17.4
1999	7 448.0	7.2	20.7
1998	6 949.0	9.2	29.4
1997	6 365.9	7.7	41.2
1996	5 991.5	7.6	50.1
1995	5 493.5	1.8	63.7
1994	5 396.2	4.7	66.6
1993	5 154.2	5.8	74.4
1992	4 871.0	1.4	84.6
1991	4 803.2	-4.4	87.2
1990	5 021.8	-0.2	79.0
1989	5,033.4	12.9	78.6
1988	4,458.4	4.8	101.7
1987	4,252.9	12.6	111.4
1986	3,778.0	0.8	138.0
1985	3,749.4	-0.4	139.8

Source: Motion Picture Association of America (2005a).

Interrelated media consumption trends

Historically, explanations for declining cinema revenues have revolved around competing technologies. Television in the 1950s and 1960s, and video recordings in the 1970s and 1980s were seen initially to be undermining cinema markets, but eventually created additional markets for cinema products. Information from Nielsen Entertainment (see MPAA 2005a, 2005c) suggests that there is a highly complex relationship between cinema attendance, which basically is the 'live performance' of a motion picture, and its subsequent consumption via broadcast or recording. The Nielsen figures indicate that:

- Satisfaction with the cinema product is high (81%).
- About one-fourth of cinema-goers plan subsequently to purchase a DVD of the film.
- Individuals who attend the cinema most frequently are also the highest investors in new home entertainment products – they account for more than 90% of DVD player sales and more than 80% of big screen TV and home cinema systems sales.

This information suggests that consumers generally do not always substitute one form of consumption with another. Rather, they use different technologies to expand their range of viewing options. This is reflected in the current revenue models of the industry in which sell-through earnings (sales of videos and DVDs directly to consumers) are now large. But this widening of consumption options also means that each filmed product must now compete in several different markets, which likewise is reflected in the current overall structure of the industry.

Film and video products and the commercial environment for digital content distribution

Online distribution of film products is an attractive prospect for telecom and cable companies that provide broadband networks. As bandwidth requirements are very high for these products, online distribution is potentially a large source of new revenue for the network operators. But depending upon the mode of delivery, these products may have different data requirements. Products such as online games typically have high data *latency* requirements, where rapid response times are required by the progress of the game. In contrast, film and video files are very large, and in some electronic transport modes may require a higher degree of *symmetry* between the uplink and downlink capacities of the telecommunications system, especially where files are exchanged on a peer-to-peer basis.

Furthermore, a very large and increasing portion of film and video content is being produced by studios that are owned by large, multinational media conglomerates. Most of these conglomerates now have substantial Internet-based undertakings in their portfolios, ranging from commercial portals and online broadcasting to cable television and telecommunication networks. The economic characteristics of high-speed digital networks are generating many new questions regarding established value chains and business models in these industries and how they will respond to evolution in digital content.

Chapter 2

FILM AND VIDEO PRODUCTION AND MARKETS IN OECD COUNTRIES

This chapter begins with an overview of some of the economic characteristics of the film and video industry that may offer challenges and opportunities for digital content markets. This is followed by an overview of current film and video markets globally, with particular focus on OECD countries, in terms of domestic production, co-production, import/export profiles and exhibition trends.

Characteristics of the film and video industry[8]

Each filmed product is in some sense an individual entity, meaning that within certain general parameters each film generates its own individual market dynamics. Virtually all film projects require large, high-risk investments and most films, even critically successful ones, fail to yield substantial returns. Moreover, the intellectual property structure of a film venture is extraordinarily complex, with different IP holders invested at many different junctures in the production sequence, each with independently negotiated rights agreements that may or may not be known to all of the other stakeholders.

'Experience' goods

The primary source of such uncertainty and instability is that films are '*experience goods*', meaning that it is not possible for consumers to determine their value until they have been consumed. In the conventional cinema environment, the number of consumers who experience the product is limited by capital investment in exhibition facilities – expressed as the number of cinema screens. In order to maximise its economic potential,

8. Unless otherwise noted, the discussion in this section has been based upon materials contained in three standard references (Caves 2000; Hoskins *et al.* 1997; and Vogel 2006) with additional reference to Deband & Chetrit (2001) regarding economic particulars specific to the European film industry.

feedback about each new cinema product must emerge and circulate quickly. In the television environment, programs must deliver high early viewer statistics in order to raise the prices of advertising slots. Whether in cinema or television mode, however, every filmed product must contend with increasing opportunity costs for the consumer, who is faced with an already large and rapidly diversifying array of media products.

Unlike most industrial products whose market characteristics often can be improved by more investment (better design, new features, etc.), it is usually not possible to 'fix' a film that has failed to attract consumers by adding further investment, except perhaps with additional promotion and advertising. Moreover, as consumer prices for filmed entertainment are relatively fixed, the more a film costs, the more consumers it will have to find. Also, production costs are not necessarily related to the size of the market. It may cost just as much to produce a film that will appeal to a very select audience as it does to make one that will appeal to a broad audience. Thus, securing distribution agreements in as many national markets as possible is essential if films with highly segmented audiences are to be profitable.

Production costs for major productions have traditionally been recovered in the producer's home market, with profits generated by foreign sales and eventually by television exhibition and sell-through merchandise such as DVDs. In this regard, films that require no obvious connection with an identifiable actor or with a specific language or cultural context (*e.g.* special effects or animated films) may be more accessible to a global audience and offer more direct links to subsidiary markets for computer games, merchandising and so forth. Indeed, the increasing use of special effects and animated sequences may signal a return to the earliest product model for filmed entertainment, which offered consumers the sensory experience of moving images that largely were free of narrative or dramatic associations.

Pricing

The quality of a film product generally is not reflected in its price. Box office prices are relatively uniform and with few exceptions follow a pre-determined price structure. Ticket prices do not go up or down on the basis of whether a new production is a 'hit' or a 'flop'. The exception concerns the revenue split between the producer and the exhibitor, which can vary throughout the exhibition cycle – typically a greater share being paid to the producer in the first part of the cycle, the balance inverting in favour of the exhibitor over the remainder of the cycle. The main way to increase revenue is to attract more viewers, and/or to export the film to another cinema market, and/or to exhibit it in another media such as television or DVD. But price discrimination opportunities within these environments can be limited as well. Pay-per-view, for example, is a model akin to the box office and package rates (subscriptions) generally do not make quality discriminations. Likewise, DVD price spreads tend not to be wide and are based mostly on the time interval between DVD release and cinema or television release.

Cost structures

Film production has high fixed and sunk costs. Irrespective of how widely the film is distributed and how many consumers purchase the product in various media, the production costs will be the same. Very few of the assets that are created or acquired for one production can be re-used in another. Furthermore, as film projects accumulate costs on a progressive basis most of the costs for each segment are sunk. If the production comes to a halt for any reason, the costs incurred to that point cannot be recovered or transferred to another production. If an option to proceed is not taken up, all previous investment is sunk.

In general, filmed entertainment products have high 'first copy' costs and much lower marginal costs, similar to electronic information services or software. However, marginal costs for analogue distribution are not negligible. Cinema prints are costly to produce and distribute and they wear out quickly. Moreover, marginal costs actually go up as the film becomes more successful (particularly the longer it runs), simply because more prints must be made and distributed (Husak 2004).

Production values

In one of the earliest published economic analyses of the film industry, Cassady (1933) illustrated how the adoption of dramatic narrative increased film production values rapidly during the industry's first couple of decades. Consumer satisfaction remains closely tied to production values. For example, with each generation of special effects-intensive films, consumers will not be satisfied with less realistic effects (except for purposefully made parodies). These rising consumer expectations place additional upward pressures on costs. Although higher production values do not necessarily ensure a more successful film, lower values may well ensure failure, and there are concomitant upward pressures on advertising and promotional costs. Moreover, workers in the creative segments – performers, directors, designers, etc. – naturally seek the highest production values possible. Realising their vision requires co-ordination of a huge quantity and variety of production inputs, involving ranked assessment of individual contributors, from stars to catering staff. The best workers are scarce and command the highest fees, thus putting further upward pressure on costs.

Managing risk

The economics of the film industry revolve around the need to protect large investments by managing risk. This involves aggregation, marketing and production strategies. The conventional way to control and co-ordinate production risks has been to aggregate production activities in one location. Thus, the US industry is clustered in Los Angeles, the UK industry in London and the French industry in Paris. But positive effects from clustering are now mostly confined to project development, financial, marketing and distribution. Many 'Hollywood' films are no longer filmed in Hollywood – often taking advantage of location shooting incentives (tax breaks and subsidies), often in other countries. But arguably the markets for these films are still created in the Hollywood cluster.

Marketing strategies aim to manage risk by increasing consumer confidence in each new film product. Typically this strategy is embodied in 'reputation-based' methods. For example, films can be produced in series which share some of the same characters and situations. The *James Bond* series is an extreme example spanning over 40 years, but many 'action' and 'fantasy' films now generate sequels. Moreover, sequels may be shot simultaneously (*e.g. Superman I* and *II* in the 1970s and more recently the *Lord of the Rings* trilogy). The most common *reputation* device has been the 'star system' which encourages serial consumption of films in which a particular performer appears. Under the old studio contract system, performer costs usually were fixed in a multi-film exclusive contract. Currently few stars are under long-term contracts and generally these now ensure only exclusive availability to a studio, the performer's fee being negotiated on a project-by-project basis. The recent termination of the arrangement between actor Tom Cruise and Paramount Studios is perhaps indicative that once star fees reach a certain proportion of production costs, studios begin to see diminishing returns (*Financial Times* 2006a and 2006b; see also Albert 1999; and De Vany and Walls 1999).

The most generally applicable production-based approach is to spread the economic risk over several projects. This strategy does not differ substantially from a typical venture capital strategy whereby a portfolio of start-up companies will be assembled under the assumption that the 'winners' cannot be selected in advance. A film investment portfolio is very similar – of every ten films, two are expected to earn high revenues, three are expected to cover costs and the remainder are expected to lose money. But this model is possible only where the domestic market is large enough to permit a steady flow of productions in reasonably high volumes, and at costs that can be recouped over the whole portfolio. New ways of spreading financial risk are also developing, based on financing films in options markets, which in turn relies on appropriate IPR protection to help ensure returns on successful ventures to investors (see Caves 2000 and Phillips 2004).

Overview of film and video markets in OECD countries

It has been noted already that cost recovery and profit generation for most filmed entertainment products typically requires that these products be exploited in several forms and in both domestic and export markets. For example, the two highest grossing features of 2005 were *Star Wars III* (US) and *Harry Potter and the Goblet of Fire* (US/UK). Each film earned worldwide box office revenues (*i.e.* excluding revenues from secondary and tertiary markets such as TV distribution, syndication, DVD sales and merchandise) of nearly USD 900 million each, more than half of which was earned in export markets (EAO 2005). As shown in Figure 2.1, foreign box office receipts for films from the major US studios and their affiliates now averages more than 50% of total box office receipts. Additionally, although figures fluctuate from film to film, at an average DVD unit price of USD 21, all of the top 20 sell-through (DVD) titles in 2005 earned on average as much or more on DVD sell-through than they did at the box office (MPAA 2005a).

Accordingly, the film and video marketplace has become highly diversified. Filmed-entertainment products can be sold in cinema box office markets, television markets (incorporating cable, satellite and broadcast segments), consumer markets (incorporating home video sales and rentals) and in online markets (incorporating Internet-based video services, interactive television and wireless digital content). Also, there are many auxiliary merchandising markets related to film and video products – toys, books, music, recordings, games, etc. All of these markets are increasingly important to the overall profitability of film-related media enterprises, but market diversification also raises many challenges with respect to capturing and holding the attention of consumers.

Figure 2.1. US plus foreign shares of box office receipts for films from major US studios and their affiliates, 2000-2005 (in USD billions)

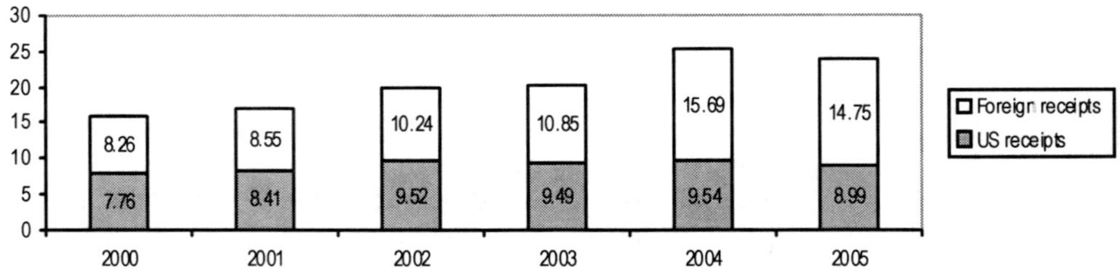

Source: MPAA (2005c).

Film-based products and the distribution of consumer media time

Table 2.1 compares the consumption of film-based media products in the US with the consumption of other media, according to the time spent by consumers with each medium per year. The relatively low position of the box office market in this table is explained easily as relatively few people actually see any given film in the cinema. However, in part due to initial promotion and advertising expenditures, cinema release becomes in effect a launch platform which is essential if the film is eventually to find its way into other media or to generate merchandising opportunities.

Table 2.1 indicates that television in its various forms is now overwhelmingly the choice of most consumers for viewing film products. Internet use is as yet modest compared to television, although consumer use of the Internet occupies a much higher portion of time than do either home video viewing or cinema attendance. Also, Internet users are presented with a much wider array of activities than are available in any other environment. Although interactive TV and wireless online services appear to have increased dramatically in only a few years, they still take up a very minor portion of consumer time devoted to the consumption of film and vide products. This may indicate continued consumer preference for established media (taking into account that pay-television and video-on-demand are available from cable networks also), or merely that the quantity of high quality Internet-based outlets is not yet sufficient.

Although the data in Table 2.1 contrast consumption of film-based and non-film-based products, it is significant that some of the 'other' media may be associated closely with film and video products. For example, consumers may acquire sound track recordings, compilations of songs that were featured in a film, books derived from a film screenplay, books upon which a screenplay was based, or video games based upon or linked to film characters and situations. Likewise, radio and press products are heavily exploited in film promotion.

Table 2.1. Yearly consumption of various media products in the United States (in hours per person)

	2001	2002	2003	2004	2005p
Filmed entertainment					
Cable and satellite TV	744	800	847	868	869
Broadcast TV	744	719	696	678	679
Consumer Internet	131	147	164	176	183
Home video[1]	47	57	60	67	76
Box office	13	14	13	12	12
Interactive TV and wireless[2]	-	4	7	11	15
Subtotal	**1 679**	**1 741**	**1 787**	**1 812**	**1 834**
Other entertainment					
Radio	952	991	1003	986	978
Recorded music	229	200	184	185	179
Newspapers	197	194	192	188	183
Magazines	127	125	121	124	124
Books	106	109	109	108	106
Video games	66	70	75	77	78
Subtotal	**1 677**	**1 689**	**1 684**	**1 688**	**1 648**
Total	**3 356**	**3 430**	**3 471**	**3 480**	**3 482**

1. Playback of pre-recorded Videocassettes and DVDs.
2. Wireless content not including pay-per-view and video-on-demand (included in cable & satellite services).
Source: Adapted from Veronis Suhler Stevenson, published in MPAA (2005a)

Cinema markets

The reported output of US, Japanese, EU, Canadian, Australian and Korean film production (films produced and/or released) amounted to over 2 000 units in 2005 (complete comparable figures for yearly production are not available for all OECD countries). Table 2.2 shows the distribution of this output by country or region of origin.

Table 2.2. Motion picture unit output for 2005 in OECD countries (excluding Mexico, New Zealand and Turkey) and closely allied countries

Country/region	Films produced and/or released	Remarks
EU	798	Closest estimate of films produced
US	699	Includes only films released
Japan	356	Includes only films released
Canada	183	Films produced and co-produced
Korea	87	Includes only films released
Australia	31	Films produced and co-produced
Total	**2 148**	

Note: The EU production figure includes EU members that are not OECD members, but their production is a very small proportion.

Source: Adapted from EAO (2005) and additional statistics from the Korean Film Council.

Figure 2.2 illustrates the historical output trends for the three largest OECD producing countries or regions – the US, EU and Japan. Overall production has not increased on average, although there have been significant fluctuations in US production from year to year and a steady small rise in both EU and Japanese production. Aggregate EU production overtook that of the US in 2000. But production *value* is considerably larger for US-produced films than for EU-produced films because of the large differences in average investment per production.

Table 2.3 gives estimates of global film and video output based upon geographical (and in some cases linguistic) distributions, along with indications as to the primary export markets for each cluster. As shown in Table 2.3[9], the English-language cluster produces a large proportion of the films that achieve virtually immediate world-wide distribution. Many contractual and co-production arrangements are undertaken between countries in this cluster. In contrast, most of the other cluster markets are primarily domestic. Where co-productions or exports occur, these are based mainly on historical links (*e.g.* between France and Africa or Spain and Latin America), cultural links (for example, the Turkish diaspora in Europe), geographical proximity, and political agreement (for example, concerning the EU).

9. Owing to the focus on OECD countries, these clusters are described in Table 2.3 in a very highly aggregated form. In particular the Asian cluster breaks down into several clusters (South Asian, Australasian and so forth) and that combining Africa and the Middle East reflects only the Arabic language segment. Some of the former Soviet Republics (the Russian Federation, Ukraine, Belarus, etc.) also constitute a cluster based in the Russian and related Slavic languages.

Figure 2.2. Yearly production of cinema films in the US, the EU and Japan, 1995-2005

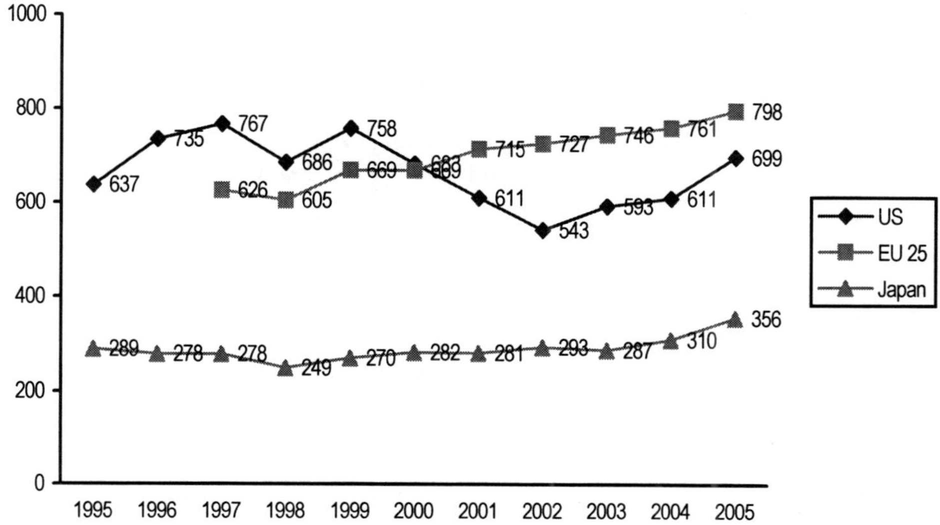

Source: EOS (2005).

Table 2.3. Feature film production and consumption clusters in the OECD

Cluster	Value share estimate*	OECD countries in each cluster	Export link sequence
English language	45%	Australia, Canada, Ireland, New Zealand, UK, US	English language, *World*
Asian	20%	Japan, Korea	Asian, English language, Western European, *World*
Latin	15%	Mexico, Portugal, Spain	Latin, Western European, English language, *World*
Western European	10%	Austria, Benelux, France, Germany, Italy, Greece, Switzerland	Western Europe, English language, Africa-Middle East, *World*
Africa-Middle East	7%	Turkey	Western European, *World*
Eastern European	2%	Czech Republic, Hungary, Poland, Slovak Republic	Eastern European, Western European, English language, *World*
Nordic	1%	Denmark, Finland, Iceland, Norway, Sweden	Nordic, Western European, English language, *World*

*Adapted from EAO (2005) and UNESCO (2005). The clusters in this table are listed in rank order according to approximate estimates of relative shares of world industry value. Market shares are intended only to give a general indication of the relative share of each of these clusters. In some clusters the countries producing much of this value are not OECD members (for example, India, China and Indonesia in the Asian cluster and Egypt, Israel and Iran in the Middle East cluster. Russia's ethnic diversity spans the Western European, Eastern European and Asian clusters.

Although selected films from any of these clusters achieve extensive international distribution on occasion, most tend only to exploit domestic and neighbouring markets. Furthermore, when seeking international distribution, many producers use the extensive international distribution capabilities of distributors that are headquartered the English-language cluster.

Table 2.4. Sources of cinema films exhibited in 2005 in selected OECD countries plus China, India and the Russian Federation

	Sources			
	Domestic	EU	US	Others
Australia	2.8%	11.6%[a]	81.2%	4.3%
Canada	4.6%	-	86.7%[b]	8.7%[c]
France	36.8%	-	45.9%	17.2%
Germany	17.1%	-	-	82.9%[d]
Italy	24.7%	12.5%[e]	53.3%	9.5%
Japan	41.3%	-	-	58.7%
Korea	55%	2.3%	38.8%	3.9%
Spain	17%	20%	60%	3%
UK	33%[f]	-	-	67%[g]
US	86%	11.6%	n/a	2.4%
China	60%	-	-	40%
India	92.5%	-	-	7.5%
Russian Federation	27.7%	6.7%	62.6%	2.9%

a. Mainly UK imports.
b. Includes US-Canada co-productions and contract productions.
c. Canada has both English and French-language markets, but the import of French-language films from the forms a small part of this figure.
d. Presumably includes imports from other EU countries, but also substantial US imports.
e. Mainly UK imports.
f. Includes UK-US co-productions.
g. Although the ethnic film market in the UK is significant, the greatest portion of this figure is likely US imports.
Source: Adapted from European Audiovisual Observatory figures (EAO 2005).

Table 2.4 illustrates that with the exception of Japan and Korea, all of the selected OECD countries are substantial importers of film content from outside their own clusters. US products overwhelmingly have the largest market share in the English-language cluster. In Canada, where there are both English and French-language markets, US films have also a substantial share of the French-language market. Of the top 20 top grossing films in Quebec in 2005, 14 were US productions or co-productions, but the rest were indigenous Quebec productions. Quebec imports relatively few productions from other French-speaking countries. In EU countries, US products have approximately a 60% market share.

Of the non-OECD countries in Table 2.4, the Indian domestic market is huge, and is expanding into international markets in Europe, North America, Africa and parts of Asia and Australasia. This is due in part to the large Indian diaspora, but also to the increasing worldwide popularity of Indian films (particularly the "Bollywood" genre). Moreover, incidences of co-production between Indian and foreign producers are increasing (see Box 2.1 and Appendix B).

Box 2.1. The film industry in India and China

India has the largest film industry in the world in terms of the number of films made and distributed. In 2004 (the latest year for which figures are available) 934 films were certified for release (as compared to 611 in the US). India is one of the few countries (the US and China are others) with a domestic market large enough for the high and consistent turnover of new film products necessary both to dominate its own domestic market and induce exports. In 2004, Indian films held a 92.5% share of the domestic market (EAO 2005). However, owing to admission prices generally averaging less than USD 0.25, earnings are relatively low. In 2004, the entire production of Indian studios was only about USD 700 million in total box office sales.

The Chinese population is marginally larger than that of India but there are many more cinema screens (about 39 000 in China to only about 12 000 in India). The enormous Chinese diaspora is a huge additional potential export market. However, production of feature films is still relatively low in China and only 260 films were released in 2005 (with one-tenth the population, Japan produced over 350 films in the same year). A diminishing share of Chinese-language production (about 20-25%) now comes from state-owned studios. The clear trend is towards production and co-production by private companies or co-production between private and publicly owned studios. An increasing number of Chinese films are co-produced with studios and investors based outside of China (mainly in the US and Canada) and some recent high production value Chinese films have found export success outside of the Chinese-language community. China imports more films per year (about 40%) than does India (about 10%) but the import market is restricted by quotas that allow no more than 20 imports per year per country of origin. Nevertheless, in the Hong Kong, China exhibition market (Hong Kong being the centre of the export industry) domestic and co-produced films earn respectable box office revenues when compared to earnings from foreign blockbusters. In 2005, earnings from the top eight imports were about USD 212 million whereas domestically produced and co-produced films earned about USD 148 million, only about 30% less (EAO 2005).

The increasingly significant incidence of international co-production complicates debates on film exports and trade. Several of the top grossing films of 2005 were international co-productions with US studios; for example, *King Kong* (US/New Zealand), *The Aviator* (US/Japan) and *The Fantastic Four* (US/Germany). Extensive historical production links between major Hollywood studios and various production companies in the UK routinely produce blockbuster hits, including four of the top 20 grossing films world-wide in 2005.

Co-production also shapes domestic markets. For example, before *ca.* 1980 Canada was an insignificant producer even of domestic content, but is now a significant exporter of film and video products (*ca.* USD 600 million in 2005), mostly contracted productions for US studios (Statistics Canada 2006). Similarly, in the major EU film-producing countries (the UK, France, Italy, Spain and Germany), on average between one-third and one-half of all productions were co-productions – largely with US studios in the case of the UK and with other EU-based production companies for the other countries (EAO 2005). In the Canadian case, there has been a large corresponding increase in production for the domestic market – co-productions and contracts are only about a third of total industry value (CFTPA 2005). A similar situation is found in the UK, although the highest value productions tend to be co-productions with US companies.

Figure 2.3. Cinema admissions in the EU, US and Japan, 1995-2005 (in millions)

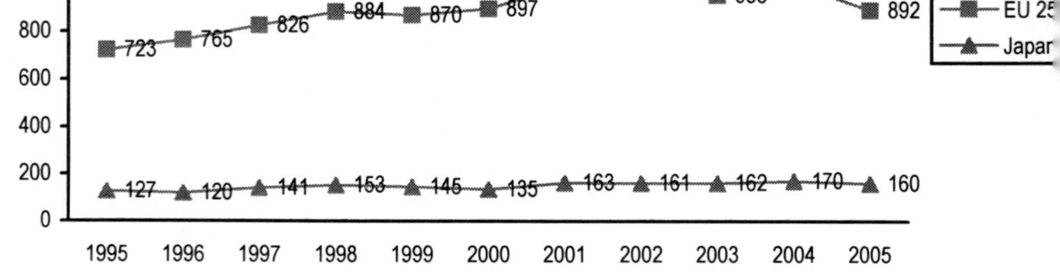

Source: EOS (2005).

Recent general trends respectively in admissions, ticket prices and cinema screens in the major US, EU and Japanese markets are given in Figures 2.3, 2.4 and 2.5. Figure 2.3 illustrates that in the US and the EU there has been a downward trend in cinema attendance since 2002, most markedly in the US. However, as shown in Table 1.1, the overall pattern in the US market is for box office revenues to fluctuate significantly from year to year, and it is not yet clear if there is a sustained downward trend.

Figure 2.4. Average ticket prices in the EU, US and Japan, 1995-2005

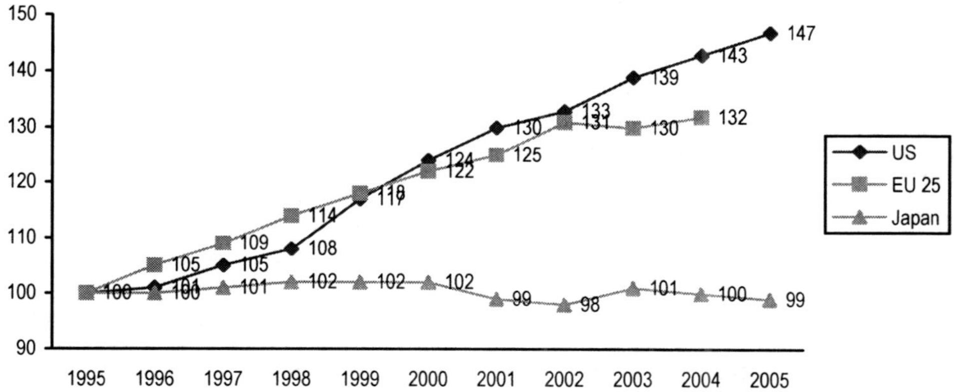

Base 100 in 1995 (calculated in national currency).
Source: EOS (2002).

Figure 2.5. Number of cinema screens in the EU, US and Japan, 1995-2005

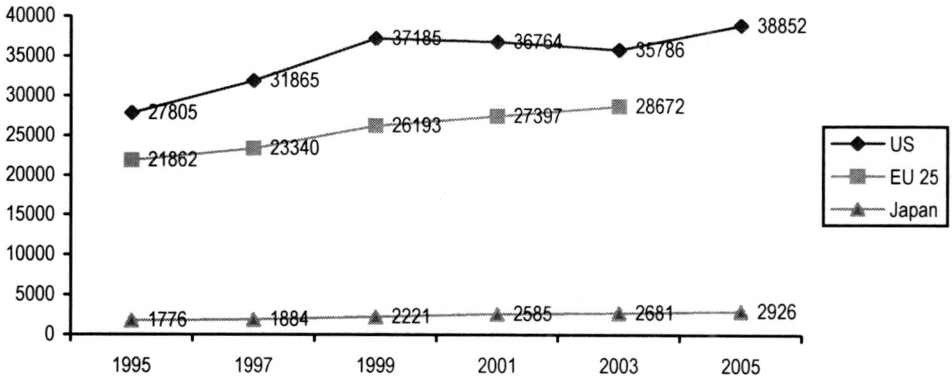

Source: EOS (2005).

What seems certain, however, is that admission figures are not affected by rises in prices. As shown in Figure 2.4, ticket prices have risen steadily every year since 1985 despite often wide fluctuations in box office receipts. Moreover, as indicated in Figure 2.5, the overall trend in the major markets since 1995 has been for the number of screens to increase quite dramatically, currently standing at their highest historical level.

Television markets

The market for television programming is similar in many respects to the cinema film market but there are several special circumstances:

- In most OECD countries there is still significant public ownership of television broadcasting. Public broadcasters contribute to increasing the overall stock of domestically produced programming, whereas private broadcasters are often more dependent on imported programs.
- Much of the television market is split between 'stock' and 'flow' programming. Most 'flow' programming (with the notable exception of live sports) is almost entirely of interest to domestic and sometimes neighbouring markets (*e.g.* Dutch-language 'flow' programming in the Netherlands and Belgium, and Swedish programming in Scandinavia).
- Cinema films make up much of television content (particularly in satellite, cable and pay-TV).
- Television broadcasts use a variety of network infrastructures (terrestrial, cable and satellite) and commercial models – advertising-supported, pay-TV, subscription cable and hybrid models.

The *production* environment for television programs is largely the same as for cinema films. Historically, however, television programs have been seen to have a much closer relationship with advertisers, the television *product* being seen more in terms of broadcast *time* rather than programming as such. In today's market, however, films too generate significant revenues from advertising, mostly in the form of product placements (see Chapter 4). Nevertheless, the proliferation of television channels has fragmented this market; where too many channels chase the same advertisers, the price of advertising time can be depressed. The reverse is true for channels that attract a high concentration of viewers.

Programming originating in the English-language cluster dominates most of the OECD markets with the exception of Mexico, Turkey, Japan and Korea. Figure 2.6 indicates the sources of broadcast fiction programming in the EU in 2000, which includes all of the European OECD countries (the non-OECD members constituting a very small total share of this market). As with the cinema markets, most programs (about 70%) are sourced from the US. For the EU, this is a comparable percentage of US imports to that of cinema markets. However, other English-language producers (the UK, Canada, Australia and New Zealand) also account for nearly 10% of the market and many products in the co-production and 'other' categories originate in or involve stakeholders in the English-language cluster. More recent figures indicate a slight upward trend in television fiction produced in the five largest EU countries, but this continues to represent a very small proportion of total television broadcast time (EAO 2005).

Figure 2.6. Trends in media usage in the OECD area (as a percentage of the total market)

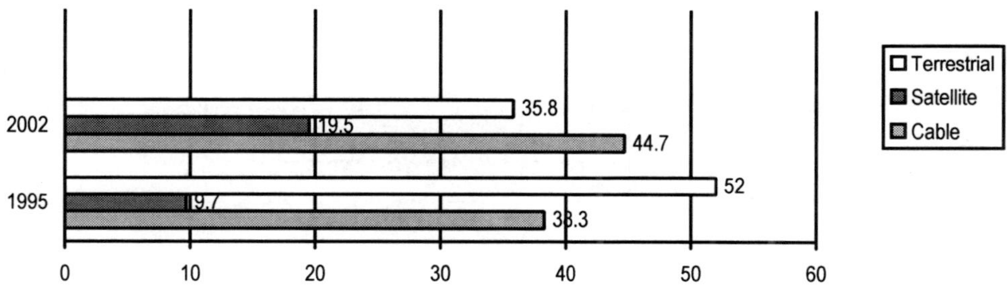

Source: OECD (2005).

Germany and the UK are the largest and most stable European fiction producers whereas Spanish production has declined substantially with that of Italy and France fluctuating within a consistent band. However, the effect of public broadcasters in this mix is substantial. Overall figures indicate that with minor fluctuations, about 60% of fiction programming in the EU as a whole is produced by public broadcasters, some of which is procured from private production companies (EAO 2005).

In the EU television industry between 1999 and 2003, digital program packaging was the highest growth segment and was beginning to show profitability. Growth was minimal in conventional public broadcasting and advertising-supported content. Growth in thematic TV companies leveled out during this period, but the profitability picture remains unstable. Likewise, home shopping undertakings showed no growth, but seemed to be showing higher profitability (Lange 2005).

Virtually all of the new digital service environments are predicated upon cable or satellite access although terrestrial digital broadcasting is significant in some markets (notably the UK). Figures 2.6 and 2.7 show clearly that whereas cable has largely supplanted terrestrial transmission of analogue broadcast signals, most access to digital TV signals in the OECD up to 2003 was via satellite. But this forms a relatively small portion of the overall access market in the OECD area. Satellite penetration is less than 30% of the total market in all but six OECD countries, the OECD average being 19.5%. However, in only two years, penetration has increased substantially in selected markets – up from zero to 22.3% in Hungary, from 12.3% to 22.2% in Ireland, from 16.6% to 22.6% in New Zealand, and from 9.9% to 28.1% in Switzerland (OECD 2005).

Figure 2.7. Digital TV households in the OECD area (as a percentage of total TV households)

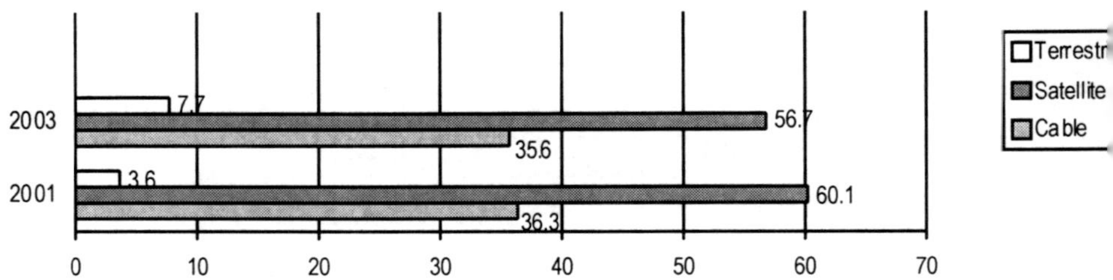

Source: OECD (2005).

However, Figure 2.8 shows that the overall growth of digital TV households has been steady in the US and Europe since 1999, particularly in Europe. Although the two are not necessarily connected, growth in digital TV households has been paralleled by growth in 'subscription' segments of the television market, indicating perhaps a growing consumer preference for enhanced or premium services (see Figure 2.9).

Figure 2.8. Growth of digital TV households

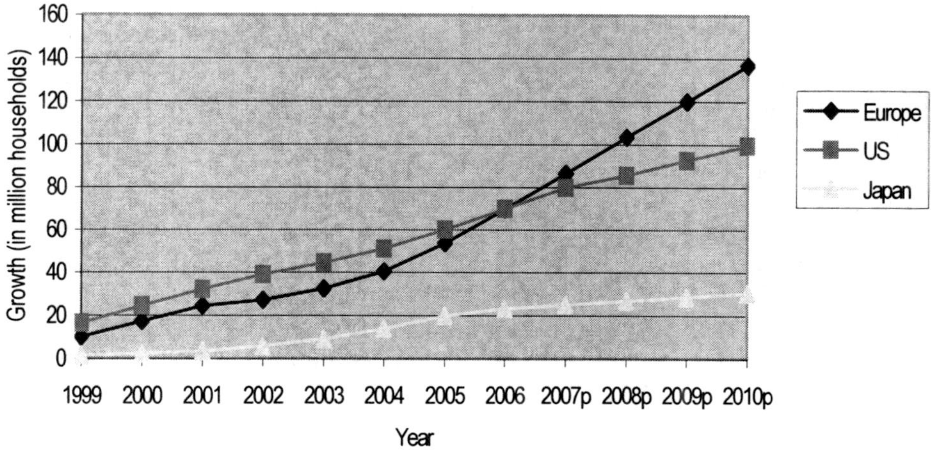

Source: Adapted from 2006 data supplied by IDATE.

Figure 2.9. Growth of subscription fees as percentage of total audiovisual markets

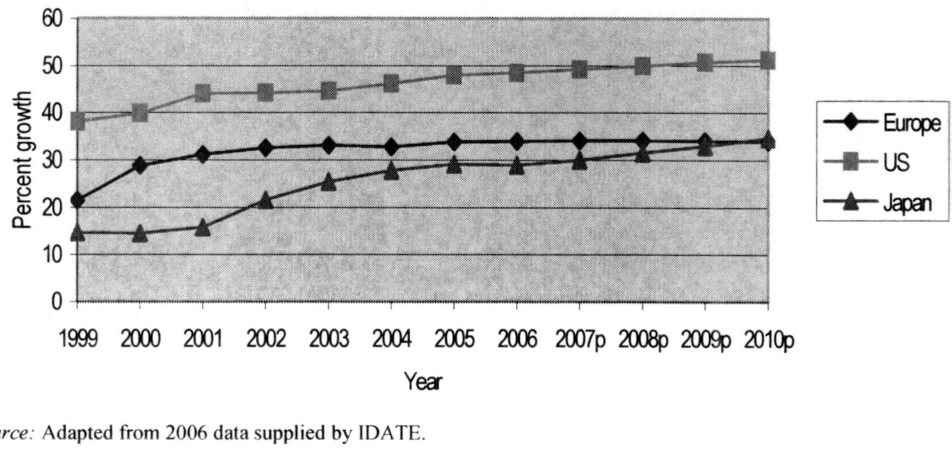

Source: Adapted from 2006 data supplied by IDATE.

Consumer video markets

Direct sales – 'sell-through' – of film and video products to consumers is now a crucial part of the revenue structure. Most cinema films earn as much or more in sell-through than they do at the box office and many original television programs appear also in sell-through markets. However, as video recordings are easy to replicate and distribute, counterfeiting becomes a major problem (see OECD 2007a). The potential for expanded home consumption appears to be tied closely to the development and uptake of more advanced home cinema technologies. As of 2005, a relatively small share of US households were intensive users of this technology and as noted in Chapter 1, use appears to be supplemental to cinema consumption.

Table 2.5. Conversion from VCR to DVD consumption in the US market, 1980-2005

Year	VCR penetration	DVD penetration	DVD player sales	DVD titles
2005	97.7 m	84.0 m	36.7 m	45 000
2004	98.9 m	65.4 m	37.1 m	40 000
2003	98.4 m	46.7 m	33.7 m	29 000
2002	97.6 m	38.8 m	25.1 m	20 000
2001	96.2 m	24.8 m	16.6 m	13 000
2000	88.1 m	-	9.9 m	8 500
1999	-	-	3.5 m	5 000
1998	-	-	0.9 m	1 500
1990	65.4 m	-	-	-
1980	1.9 m	-	-	-

Source: Derived from Adams Media, Nielsen Media, Phillips Business Information and Digital Entertainment Group data.

Tables 2.5 and 2.6 illustrate the speed and magnitude of the crossover from VHS to DVD. Furthermore, the advent of the DVD has rapidly expanded the market (although there are some signs of flattening out). This growth is due in part to the greater convenience of the new format, and the opportunity for consumers to increase the quality of home consumption by buying up to more advanced home cinema technologies.

Table 2.6. Conversion from VHS to DVD entertainment products in the US, 2001-2005 (in millions of items)

	VHS			DVD		
	Rent	Sell-through	Total	Rent	Sell-through	Total
2005	14.9	33.7	**48.6**	178.4	1 114.2	**1 292.6**
2004	33.9	115.7	**148.7**	149.1	1 063.2	**1 212.3**
2003	53.2	240.2	**293.4**	110.9	768.2	**879.1**
2002	73.6	407.5	**481.1**	79.3	539.9	**619.2**
2001	86.2	539.6	**625.8**	37.1	313.9	**351.0**

Source: Adams Media Research.

Online video markets

Online video markets are still a developing market segment. There is also an illegal market for video downloads but our focus in this study is entirely on the legal market. Table 2.1 showed that in the 2001-2005 period Internet access to video content took up less than 10% of consumer time devoted to filmed entertainment, indicating a still infant market segment. However, Figure 2.10 shows recent market research indicating that consumers are becoming increasingly familiar with the online video environment.

Figure 2.10. Percent of consumers who are aware of or watch online video in 2006

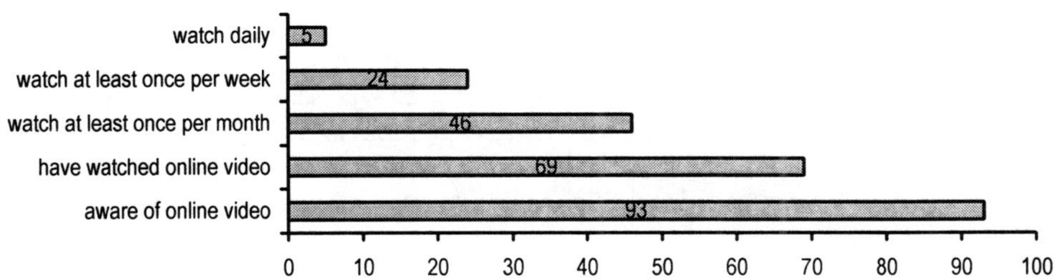

Source: Online Publishers Association.

Nevertheless, downloading as such is only one option for online distribution and the downloading environment itself has as yet no ubiquitous or homogenous business model. DVDs can also be sold or rented on e-commerce portals. In 2005, the online DVD rental market had nearly 4.5 million subscribers in the US and just under 1 million in Europe. It was projected that nearly 45 million DVDs would be delivered to European subscribers by post in 2005 and more than 380 million to US subscribers, constituting one in ten video rentals, and that in the UK over half of the video rental market would move online by 2009 (Screen Digest 2006). These projections suggest that the electronic commerce aspect of online distribution may be just as important in the short to medium term as the downloading aspect.

Table 2.7. Actual and projected online cinema product revenues, 2004-2006 (in USD millions)

	2004	2005	2006	2008p	2010p
US	9.5	11.8	22.9	454.6	1 974.5
EU	1.8	3.7	24.6	269.3	1 356

Source: EU 2006 (from *Screen Digest* data).

Earlier OECD analysis indicated that although accessing entertainment and media products now constitutes a considerable share of consumer Internet activities, evolving consumer behaviours regarding audio files have yet to be transferred substantially to the video file-sharing environment (see OECD 2004, OECD 2006a). Nevertheless, video downloading is showing signs of developing into a significant new revenue stream. Based upon trends shown in the 2004-2006 period, *Screen Digest* projects (Table 2.7) that by 2010, video downloading will have grown to just under USD 1.9 billion in the US and just over USD 1.3 billion in Europe. To put this figure into perspective, however, for the European market this figure represents only about one-sixth of either box office or DVD revenue projections, or just over one-twelfth of total projected filmed entertainment revenues for 2010 (EU 2006). The US figure would represent an even smaller proportion. Significantly, the *Screen Digest* projections for growth in the downloading segment are tied to projections that the box office and DVD markets will level off rather than go into protracted decline, reflecting the historical patterns of new media introduction whereby older media decline but do not disappear (see Chapter 1).

Chapter 3

THE EVOLVING STRUCTURE OF THE FILM AND VIDEO INDUSTRY

This chapter focuses on elements of industry structure and cost structure that are most relevant to the future of digital audio-visual content. A large share of the value added in the motion picture industry in the OECD region is produced or distributed by seven major US-based studios, and discussion of new production and distribution modalities, value chain transformation and business model development begins with these globally important producers. Furthermore, all of the major studios play an important market-making role in the global industry. However, there are many national and regional variations in industry structure and even in the United States there is significant independent production and distribution, especially on the television side.

Of the seven major Hollywood-based studio complexes, several of the largest are at present owned or have been owned at some time wholly or partly by companies headquartered outside the US – Sony (Japan), News Corporation (US headquartered since the end of 2004, but formerly headquartered in Australia) and Vivendi (France). With the purchase of Metro-Goldwyn-Mayer Inc. by a US-Japanese consortium led by Sony and Comcast, the Hollywood cluster contains only three studios that continually have been owned by US-based undertakings: Warner Bros., Paramount and Walt Disney. Thus, ownership of Hollywood assets is significantly internationalised, and the industry is a significant importer of investment capital (Phillips 2004).

In many respects, the basic structure of the Hollywood cluster appears not to have changed significantly in nearly 100 years. Cassady (1933) showed how the motion picture industry assumed a stable basic form within a remarkably short period following its inception. With the advent of filmed stories (generally considered to have begun in 1903 with *The Great Train Robbery*), consumers began to judge films more on the basis of story and production quality and very soon upon the personalities of film performers. Essentially, by about 1915, the basic elements of what became known as the 'studio system' were in place and the Hollywood of the 1920s looked much the same as it does today. The names of the major studios are still familiar – Fox, Metro-Goldwyn-Mayer, Paramount, United Artists, Warner Brothers, Universal and Columbia. Between *ca.* 1915 and 1935 a series of judicial and US Trade Commission rulings ended the vertical integration of film production with cinema exhibition. The basic principles that were established in these rulings governing relations between producers and newly independent exhibitors still apply today.

Vertical integration of the production and distribution segments was not affected by these rulings. But from the late 1950s onwards, several significant structural changes have been observable:

- Most motion picture studios have been absorbed by media conglomerates.
- The organisational structure of motion picture production has changed.
- The economic and financial structures of the industry have been re-oriented.
- Film and television market segments have been more directly linked.
- Motion picture distribution modalities and exhibition venues have been expanded and restructured.

Structural change in the film and video industry

The evolving position of motion picture products in the media industry[10]

The media environment in the OECD countries is dominated by large vertically integrated multinational conglomerates that own or have substantial interests in a wide range of audio, visual and print media and in communication networks of various kinds. Before about 1960 most major studios were wholly independent companies specializing in filmed entertainment. Since then, all of the major Hollywood production studios and television networks have become parts of much larger conglomerates. Except for CBS, all of the major US national broadcast television networks (ABC, NBC and Fox) along with broadcast television undertakings in many other OECD countries are subsidiaries of the same conglomerates that own the Hollywood studios. So are many of the cable and pay-TV networks – for example HBO, CNN, Arts & Entertainment (A&E) and ESPN.

10. Unless otherwise noted, the information in this section is taken from the 2005 Annual Reports for the relevant companies and from US Securities and Exchange Commission (SEC) filings for 2003-2005.

Thus, particularly in the market-leading English-language production bloc, most cinema films and television programs are produced and/or distributed either by subsidiaries of the seven conglomerates, or by independents working either under contract to one of the major studios or otherwise linked to their production and/or distribution facilities. In the other major production blocs – for example those centred in selected EU countries (especially France, Italy and Germany) and in Latin America – analogous relationships are common between national or regional production studios and media conglomerates of various descriptions, some of which also have interests in the major Hollywood studios.

A notable exception concerns the members of the European Union, which in accordance with the provisions of Television Without Frontiers Directive, must ensure where practicable, that public as well as private broadcasters reserve a majority proportion of their transmission time (excluding news, sports events, games, advertising, teletext services and teleshopping) for European content and at least either 10% of their transmission time or 10% of their programming budget, for European content created by producers who are independent of broadcasters. Another exception concerns public and in some cases independent private broadcasters in a few OECD countries – notably, the UK, Japan, Australia and France – that are significant producers of motion picture content for television. Particularly in the English-language bloc, it is common for public broadcasters to commission content from independent producers, many of whom often distribute and exhibit this content internationally through the major studios. For example, Film Four, the film production division of Channel Four (the UK independent not-for-profit television channel) has distributed films theatrically and on DVD through the Walt Disney Company and Sony Pictures.

Conglomerates are a feature of media industries in all OECD countries. With the exception of public broadcasters – and at least one of these (the BBC) has acquired something of the profile of a small multinational conglomerate – virtually every audio-visual media undertaking in the OECD area (and beyond) is now wholly or partly owned by one or more of perhaps 50 conglomerates based mainly in eight countries (the US, the UK, France, Germany, Italy, Canada, Australia and the Netherlands). These include the Axel Springer Group, the Bertelsman Group, Vivendi, the Berlusconi companies, the Carlton Group and the Granada Group, but most of these are much more heavily invested in print, music and networking businesses than in film and television production.

Although the major Hollywood studio and network undertakings are now structurally part of conglomerates, it is important to stress that they operate as entirely independent companies within these structures, as indeed do most of the subsidiaries in other media segments. Within each segment, markets are competitive. Indeed, as noted in Chapter 2, in many respects every individual film and video product creates its own market; consumers make choices according to the characteristics of individual film and video products and not according to which studio produced them. Moreover, as shown below, all of the conglomerates that own film and video production and distribution companies have different overall 'footprints', their businesses often reflecting the historical origins of these companies. The conglomerate phenomenon could be considered a natural outcome of a marketplace in which the rapid proliferation of new product types, often in conjunction with new technology, is fragmenting consumption patterns and shifting revenue streams from traditional to new media products.

Each of the seven major Hollywood groups is listed below along with its main subsidiary motion picture companies (wholly or partly owned, including distribution companies), and the ownership of these groups is illustrated in Figure 3.1:[11]

- *Walt Disney Pictures* – incorporating Walt Disney Pictures, Touchstone Pictures, Miramax Films, Hollywood Pictures, and Buena Vista Pictures.
- *Metro-Goldwyn-Mayer (MGM)* – incorporating MGM Pictures, United Artists Pictures and Orion Pictures Corp.
- *Sony Pictures* – incorporating the Columbia-Tristar Motion Picture Group, Columbia Pictures, Sony Pictures Classics, Screen Gems and TriStar Pictures.
- *Warner Brothers* – incorporating Castle Rock Entertainment, New Line Cinema Corp and Fine Line Features.
- *Paramount Pictures* – incorporating Paramount Classics, DreamWorks and DreamWorks Animation.
- *Twentieth Century Fox* – incorporating Fox Studios, Fox Searchlight, Fox 2000 Pictures, New Regency Films and Blue Sky Studios.
- *Universal Pictures* – incorporating Universal Studios, Focus Features, Rogue Films and Working Title Films.

11. The corporate structure of the various studio groups is complex and changeable. Divisions reorganise frequently and registered business names change. To lend some continuity and brand recognition, each studio group is identified under the most common names that for most consumers would identify film products as emanating from a particular studio group. Thus, "Warner Brothers" and "20th Century Fox" are used even though these are brand names respectively of Time Warner Entertainment and Fox Filmed Entertainment. The best-known production subsidiaries in each group are listed by corporate name.

Figure 3.1. Ownership of major studio groups

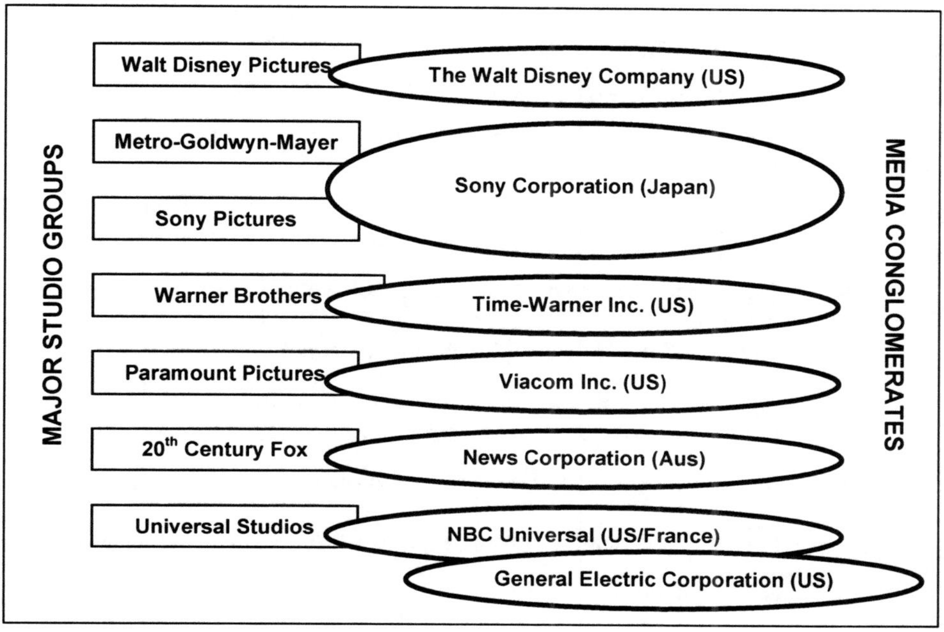

MGM has played a variety of roles in a variety of conglomerate structures – for example with Turner Communications and then Time Warner, and now with a new ownership consortium led by Sony and Comcast (a US cable television network). The NBC-Universal Group is the most recent outcome of a series of rapid mergers and acquisitions since 2000. It is now owned jointly by the General Electric Corporation (80%) and Vivendi (20%).

The product portfolios of the whole group of conglomerates are illustrated in Table 3.1, which shows that by being part of a larger media group, the studio complexes become linked to a much greater variety of media products – particularly to television (broadcast and cable) and to Internet-oriented undertakings of many kinds. The conglomerates have a particularly strong profile in broadcast and cable television. With the exception of CBS, all of the major US television networks are owned by these conglomerates as are many other broadcast networks:

- The Walt Disney Company owns the ABC Network and Touchstone Television, plus several cable channels (including the Disney Channel, ABC Family and ESPN).
- NBC Universal owns the NBC Television Network as well as various cable channels (including the History Channel, CNBC-Dow Jones and Bravo).
- Viacom owns MTV Networks, which includes, among other cable channels, MTV, VH1, and Nickelodeon, as well as BET.
- News Corporation owns the Fox Broadcasting Company and Fox Cable Networks, which includes the Fox Movie Channel, the Fox Soccer Channel and the National Geographic Channel.
- Sony does not operate broadcast television networks but is a major producer of television content through Sony Pictures Television.
- Time Warner owns the US and foreign operations of HBO and CNN.

Table 3.1. Product segment profiles of major multinational media conglomerates

	NBC-Universal	Time Warner	Viacom	Walt Disney	News Corp.	Sony Corp.
Film production	•	•	•	•	•	•
TV production	•	•	•	•	•	•
TV networks	•	•	•	•	•	•
Internet	•	•	•	•	•	•
Cable TV	•	•	•	•	•	
Merchandise	•	•	•	•		•
Theme parks	•		•	•		•
Music				•	•	•
Publishing		•	•	•	•	
Satellite TV					•	•
Telecom		•	•			•
Radio			•	•		
Cinemas			•			
Live theatre				•		
Sports					•	
Video games		•				•
Advertising		•	•		•	
Electronics						•

In addition to television channels, several conglomerates now have positions in *cable networks* that provide networking facilities as well as distribution outlets. For example, Time Warner owns Time Warner Cable and News Corporation owns cable channels in Fox Cable Networks. Cable is of course also an important broadband Internet access vehicle in many OECD markets. Although *satellite networks* are not yet significant for Internet access relative to terrestrial and mobile telecommunication networks (including cable-based telecommunication facilities), only Viacom and Walt Disney do not have current holdings in this segment. News Corporation largely pioneered Direct Broadcast Satellite services and although it is spinning off its interest in DirecTV it retains its stakes in BSkyB and its wholly owned SKY Italia subsidiary and has for example launched an Indian venture with Tata (Tata Sky).

Some of the media conglomerates that own major Hollywood studios also own cinema chains, but these chains operate at arm's length from the studios, each exhibiting products from several studios. Of the conglomerates that currently own major Hollywood studios, only Viacom and Vivendi have substantial cinema chain interests, some of them operated in joint ventures. Viacom owns Famous Players and Paramount Theatres and Vivendi retains an interest in Cineplex-Odeon. United Cinemas International is a joint venture between them. More specialised media segments (radio, live theatre, sports teams, video games, advertising and electronics) are distributed more thinly. However Sony Corporation is one of the largest suppliers in both video games and consumer electronics. Although Vivendi is no longer a major player in the Hollywood nexus, it remains one of the largest stakeholders in the video games segment.

All of the studio-owning conglomerates hold substantial interests in commercial Internet operations (ISPs or major commercial portals). Sony also has interests in various electronic device markets that have substantial relevance to digital content development and distribution on Internet platforms. The following list gives an indication of the broad range of Internet interests:

- Time Warner owns America Online (AOL), one of the world's largest Internet access facilities and many associated operations.
- The NBC Universal group provides enhanced broadcasting facilities on Internet platforms in collaboration with Intel Corp. (Intercast) and Microsoft (MSNBC). The group operates NBC Internet, CNBC Dow-Jones, and NBC desktop video, publishing and data network services.
- Viacom owns many online media concerns, mostly connected to MTV and BET.

- Disney is a major investor in online content services and claims upwards of 40 million visitors per month to its sites, including Disney.com and ABCnews.com (Disney Annual Report 2005).
- News Corporation includes Fox Interactive Media which has several Internet-oriented acquisitions including Intermix Media, MySpace and Scout Media (online sports network).
- Sony Pictures owns Sony Pictures Digital Entertainment, covering visual effects, animated entertainment and games services including Sony Online Entertainment. Outside of the US, Sony Pictures Television International owns and operates over 40 cable and satellite channels and is a leading producer of content for broadcasters. Sony Pictures Television International is also a partner in HBO channels in Central Europe, Asia, and Latin America.

Time Warner and Viacom are also operators of telecommunication networks. Time Warner operates Time Warner Communications, a cable-based telecommunication service. Viacom has an extensive wireless services portfolio structured around its MTV operation (*e.g.* ring tones) and cable TV. In 2005, Viacom had distribution agreements with 25 major mobile telephone networks.

Walt Disney, Time Warner and News Corporation report earnings on a reasonably comparable business segment basis. At present, about 25% of their earnings come from filmed entertainment. Sony is not comparable owing to its huge consumer electronics profile (about 75% of its total business) whereas NBC Universal is so new that comparable data are as yet unavailable. Overall and with some adjustments, it is estimated that on average, filmed entertainment contributes about 25% of media-related revenues for a typical studio-owning conglomerate. This makes the segment structurally important, but not dominant in every case. For most companies, networking businesses are now a major source of revenue (between one-quarter and two-thirds of total earnings), mainly related to TV and Internet operations. Disney, Time Warner and Viacom are already structured primarily around networking revenues and the others clearly are moving in this direction.

Because of the range of businesses in these larger groups, certainly there is scope for pursuing new value-chain configurations and business models that involve different companies in different media segments within the same conglomerate. However, given the fluidity of the product and the technological environment, it would be premature to generalise about any such strategies.

The organisational structure of film production

Film production has evolved substantially from a studio system based upon in-house production, to essentially a prime contracting system in which most of production inputs into a motion picture are outsourced. The major studios and their affiliates are now involved mainly in market development and/or distribution. The prime contractor model has led to the rise of Production Services Companies, such as Weta Digital, Alianza Films, and AKOM Studios. It has also had the effect of further integrating independent producers with the major studios. Some independent production studios, such as Medusa, Constantin, Pathé, Acorn, or ADV Films, still work outside the studio system, but the typical film is now a co-production between several affiliated or independent production companies and a major studio. Most films are produced by several different types of companies, configured on a project-by-project basis:

- *The major studios* are Walt Disney, MGM, Warner Bros, Universal, Sony, Paramount and 20th Century Fox. These studios operate in every area of film production, from intellectual property acquisition to distribution and exhibition.
- *Major studio affiliates* are production companies that are wholly or partly owned by the major studios. These include companies like DreamWorks, Miramax, Touchstone, Orion, New Line and Castle Rock. These are primarily production companies.
- *Major independent studios* are production companies like LucasFilm, or Lions Gate Films that also own or operate production facilities. In the case of LucasFilm, these facilities revolve around computer-generated special effects and production software, whereas Lions Gate operates one of the largest North American production studio facilities outside of Los Angeles (in Vancouver, Canada). These are primarily production companies who may distribute some films independently, but rely mainly on negotiated distribution agreements with major studios.
- *Independent production companies* include dozens of firms that acquire and develop literary or conceptual properties and produce motion pictures. Generally they do not own their own studio facilities, relying instead upon contracted facilities or location shooting. Many of these companies are associated with specific genres or with individual actors, producers or screenwriters. These companies can produce independently or in joint ventures with major studios or other independents. Typically their products are distributed by a major studio group.

- *Production services companies* provide technical and administrative services and facilities under contract to production companies of all types. In addition to specialised independent contractors, major and minor independent studios may provide contracted services to other (much smaller) production companies – for example, studio and post-production facilities.

As reflected in the title sequences, a typical film production project now involves a consortium of production and service companies. Typically major film studios are involved mostly in the project development, financial and final product distribution phases of the business.

Financial structures in a distributed production environment

It was noted earlier that the current investment strategy for the industry resembles more a venture capital style portfolio in which investment risks are spread over a group of films, the highest grossing units carrying the rest. However, although overall earnings from a film portfolio are still important to the studios, the market development and promotion strategy has become oriented to high-profile blockbusters that are expected to deliver much higher than average financial performance in a relatively short period. The main characteristic of a blockbuster is that it earns a lot of money in box office sales within the first week of release. The first weekend on US screens generates on average about 30% of the box office revenues from the first cinema release for a typical film. Films with relatively modest budgets, or where the budget is focused upon performers rather than effects, can sometimes outperform those with enormous budgets. For example, of the top 20 grossing films of 2005, 15 were high-budget special effects-intensive films, but five had little or no such content. Moreover, in terms of US box office receipts of films released in 2005, the modest *Wedding Crashers* did almost as well at the US box office as *King Kong*, and better than *Batman Begins*, *Fantastic Four*, and *Robots*, all of which were special effects-intensive films (EAO 2005, IMDb data base 2007).

The source of finance is becoming an increasingly complex issue. Funding directly from major studios started to decline in the mid-1980s. This was counterbalanced to some extent with co-production structures in which independent production companies assumed varying degrees of financial risk under rights-splitting arrangements. Increasingly, this may involve the export of risk to institutional (often offshore) investors using various investment instruments. Phillips (2004) suggests that this type of financing, which has involved major financial institutions (investment banks, insurance companies, options markets, etc.), may in part be compensating for the shortfall in direct finance from the major studios themselves.

A further co-financing consideration concerns the international out-sourcing of production activities. Such arrangements have perhaps the longest history between the US and the UK. Independent UK studios have been co-producing films with Hollywood majors for worldwide release since the 1930s. More recently, Canada has become a preferred Hollywood production site and similar relationships exist between producers head-quartered in Europe and Asia. McFayden *et al.* (1998) suggest several possible advantages of foreign-based co-production including pooling financial resources, access to production incentives and subsidies from foreign govern-ments, access to the national market of the co-producer or to third-country markets, acquiring rights in a film property or film-related IPR, accessing foreign locations, and reducing production costs (by utilising cheaper production crews and facilities). But they also note several drawbacks and additional risks, including higher administrative co-ordination and shooting costs for multi-country productions, and extra costs incurred by the bureaucracy associated with subsidies and incentives as provided by foreign governments. They also note the risk that in a globalising market, production skills may be transferred to potential competitors.

Convergence of film and video production

The linkage between film and video has become especially close. From at least the mid-1950s onwards, television programs (particularly dramatic series and specials) have been made using the production and technical facilities of the major studios. At first, however, these markets remained quite separate. Today's cinema and television markets are much more inter-twined. The mini-series phenomenon and the advent of original productions by pay and cable television undertakings – like HBO – raised the production values of selected television programming to those of cinema films.

Restructuring distribution and exhibition

There is currently considerable restructuring in the conventional cinema exhibition segment with the development of the multiplex format, and this is likely to undergo further change with the adoption of digital cinema (see Chapter 5). Figure 2.5 showed strong growth between 1995 and 2005 in the number of cinema screens in the largest OECD markets, but the increase in the number of films produced per year was far less pronounced. US production fluctuated considerably, on average producing more films between 1995 and 2000 than between 2000 and 2005. During this entire period, overall production increased steadily only in the EU countries and then by a modest amount.

The discrepancy can be explained largely by the increase in multiplex cinemas which not only increases the opportunity for more consumers to view a given film, but also provides new commercial strategies to cinema operators. To illustrate the penetration of multiplexes, Figure 3.2 shows multiplex cinemas in various European countries as a percentage of total screens. US data show that the number of sites has diminished significantly since 1995 but that the average number of screens per site has crept up from four to six over this period. European figures show that multiplexes dominate in only three markets, but that they had a more than 20% share in well over half the countries in this group of European countries.

Figure 3.2. Indoor cinema screens in multiplexes in selected European OECD countries 2004

As a percentage of total screens

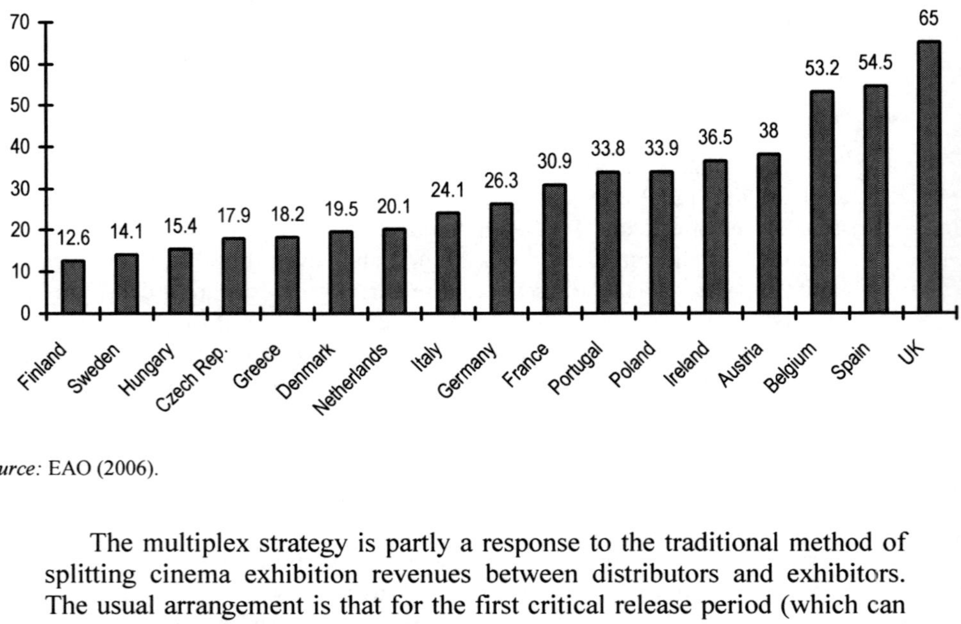

Source: EAO (2006).

The multiplex strategy is partly a response to the traditional method of splitting cinema exhibition revenues between distributors and exhibitors. The usual arrangement is that for the first critical release period (which can be defined differently for each film) the distributor takes the largest share of box office receipts. This split inverts in favour of the exhibitor the longer the film stays on release (Husak 2004). The system has advantages for distributors in that as revenues begin to decline, a film can be moved to a smaller room, and the availability of large rooms necessary to ensure opening weekend success can be guaranteed.

Although the multiplex format was developed prior to the advent of digital cinema, its characteristics are nevertheless conducive to conversion. Digital feeds create further efficiencies in redistributing a film from one room to another over its exhibition cycle – even to the point of allowing dynamic selection of rooms on a showing-by-showing basis. As shown in Figure 3.3, conversion to digital screens would seem to be picking up rapidly with more than a 150% increase between 2004 and 2005. Cost estimates for conversion vary considerably, but estimates of around USD 75 000 to 100 000 per screen are common (Husak 2004; Dettmer 2003). This may seem a modest investment, but with currently over 37 000 screens at nearly 6 000 sites in the US alone, the cost of total conversion would be enormous.

Figure 3.3. Growth in digital cinema screens worldwide, 2000-2005

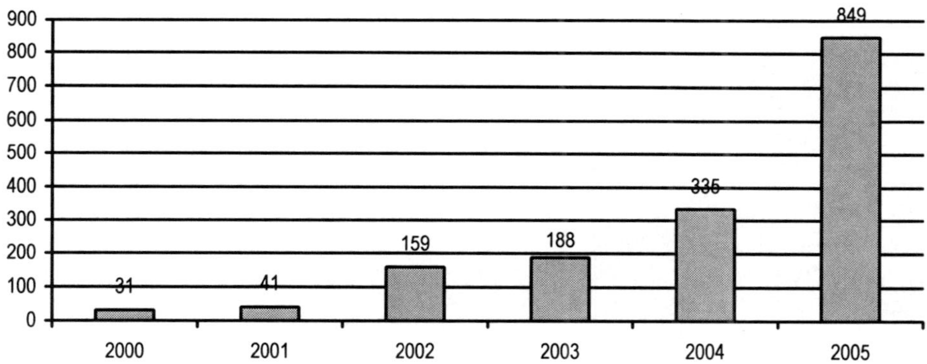

Source: MPAA (2005a).

Implications for digital content of industry structure evolution

The changes in industry structure reviewed above are very substantial and largely similar across media markets in most OECD countries. Notably, however, there would appear to be no general trend to increase the number of films released each year. Production volumes are linked to many factors including historical and projected demand, as well as to the characteristics of the various media in which various forms of content will be distributed. The most visible trend has been to promote greater capacity and efficiency in the exhibition system, extending recently to increasing investment in digital cinema as well as exploration and increasing use of digital delivery options. Cinema exhibition is still the primary portal for engaging audience and developing supplementary sell-through, television distribution and merchandising markets.

The industry both historically and currently is dependent upon preserving a delicate balance between the amount of investment in production at any given time, the amount of product that is released in any given period and the sequence of 'after-markets' that are derived from the first release of a filmed product. Thus, the most logical strategy for further exploitation of content in digital formats would appear to be in higher volume distribution of existing titles and better development of secondary and tertiary markets.

Chapter 4

THE VALUE CHAIN OF THE FILM AND VIDEO INDUSTRY

Value chains are descriptive models of the economic process of value accumulation in a given industry, starting from the lowest value input (in terms of the specific product or service) and proceeding to the highest value output. The analytical function of the value chain in this study is to indicate where and how historical value has been created, and where and how new value might be created in a digitised content environment.

The film and video industry has an especially complex value chain, both in terms of the quantity and diversity of its various segments and in terms of the nature or character of many of these segments. As an 'experience good', the realisable value of a film is determined largely by *intangible assets* that have very special characteristics. Consumer perceptions of the personality and talents of individuals associated with a film can play a crucial role in determining the value of the film. Unlike the music or publishing industries, however, these 'personality' assets are tied to an extremely varied and costly set of production and distribution processes in which value accumulates through a particularly complex interaction between tangible and intangible assets.

As digitisation of motion picture production processes and content intensifies, some segments of the value chain will be transformed. But as many of the value segments are not technological in orientation or function, their current value chain position may well not change. For many of the segments that do change in character or function, the key dynamic may not be technological substitution (the replacement of analogue media with digital media), but the exploitation of technical change in order to develop new sources of value from the filmed entertainment product.

Much of the discussion in previous sections suggests that the film product is now actually an *intermediate good.* In some cases the strategy is to establish film characters and story lines as 'brands' upon which various auxiliary sources of revenue can be constructed, irrespective of whether the films containing these characters of stories are on release or not. Although the actual share of revenues obtained through these strategies may vary, they constitute added value and as such must be incorporated into the value chain. Furthermore, in the context of digitisation, many of these auxiliary markets offer some of the most substantial opportunities to develop new goods and services based specifically upon digital content.

The value chain for filmed entertainment products

The value chain below describes a generic *filmed entertainment product* whether a cinema film or a television program. Most of the processes are practically the same regardless of the medium in which it may eventually appear, and most motion picture products appear in several media, either sequentially or simultaneously. Several of the value-added segments in the chain are either entirely digital already or otherwise have become heavily mediated by digital technology, but many value-added segments of this product grouping are still oriented to analogue media.

The value-added structure

The value chain is constructed with reference first to the lowest level value input; namely, the concept, scenario or literary property upon which the film or video is based. This subject or 'property' may exist already in some other form – for example, a published novel or television series. The first levels of value are added via investment in the *'negative'* and *'P&A'* cost streams (defined and explained in Chapter 1). Various additional investments in distribution, exhibition, merchandising and so forth add yet further levels of value. Over time, revenues from these additional investments may in many cases rival or surpass income from the cinema run. But all are contingent upon the prior existence of a film product. Thus, there are four distinct value-added streams that must be taken into consideration in the value chain model:

- *'Negative' value-added* accumulates in the production of a motion picture.
- *P&A value-added* accumulates in the distribution and promotion of a motion picture.

- *Exhibition value-added* accumulates as the motion picture is made available to consumers in various forms.
- *Auxiliary value-added* accumulates as various additional products and services are derived from the motion picture content and associated assets.

Figure 4.1. The basic motion picture investment model

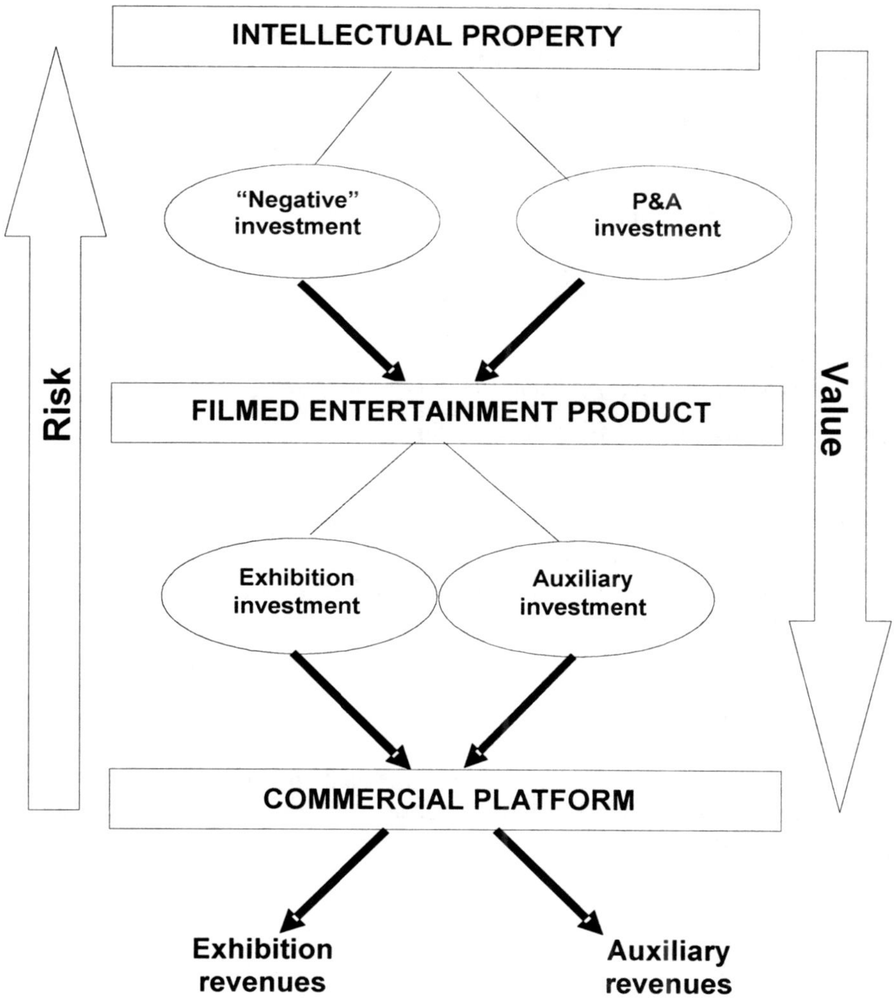

The investment sequence

As shown in Figure 4.1, investment is made first in the process of converting the intellectual property into a film. This process incurs investment costs in both the 'negative' and P&A streams. As indicated by the arrow to the left, it also involves the greatest amount of high risk capital. Once the film exists it can be converted into a much broader commercial platform. This requires further investments in both exhibition facilities and media and also in auxiliary product development. As indicated by the arrow on the right of the diagram, usually these downstream stages require lower quantities of risk capital relative to the production stages Many of these markets are exploited within already established infrastructures (as with cinema exhibition facilities or established merchandising outlets), but other investment can be specific to an individual film – *e.g.* the manufacture of spin-off merchandise (toys, clothing, games, etc.).

The value chain

From this basic model of how and where the investment capital is spent, the features of the value chain can be fleshed out. The result of this process is depicted in Figure 4.2. Importantly, the motion picture product itself appears not as the end point of the value chain, but as *the core intermediate product to which yet further levels of value can be added.*

The value chain relative to the negative and P&A streams is cumulative – each segment builds upon value added at previous (sometimes parallel) levels. However, the value-added structure of the exhibition and auxiliary streams is not so straightforward. The exhibition stream segments are depicted according to what at this point in time appear to be the most common value-added relationships and sequences. Products are made both for film and television exhibition, and in some cases, first release will be in the cinema and in other cases on television. Some products may be conceived originally for one type of release and then shifted to another. Similar crossovers can be found regarding broadcast and pay television (including video-on-demand). Both cinema and television films may be distributed on video and DVD or eventually online. At this point, usual practice is for DVD or online release to follow cinema or television release, but some products go directly to these media, bypassing cinema and television release.

Figure 4.2. The filmed entertainment value chain

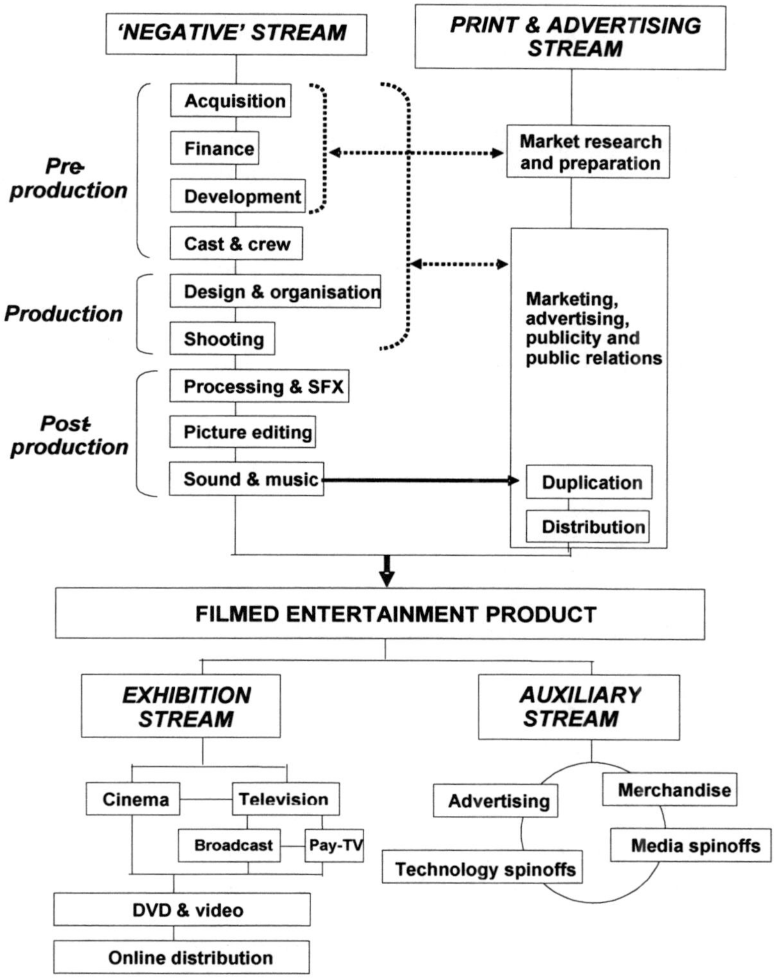

Auxiliary revenue streams are related to the film property but unrelated to exhibiting the film as such – *i.e.* they are additional to box office, television or sell-through income. Opportunities to develop auxiliary markets are normally related to the characteristics and content of individual cinema films or television programs. For example, *Star Wars* or *Indiana Jones* have proven highly conducive to generating a wide variety of merchandise and media spin-offs (a television series in the case of *Indiana Jones*). Opportunities to develop auxiliary markets from original television programming may occur somewhat less often than for cinema films, but they are also significant. Children's programming in particular is a source of auxiliary markets where merchandise often is closely tied to program characters and situations – *e.g.* the *Smurf* or *Teenage Mutant Ninja Turtle* merchandising operations. Likewise, films with a high special effects or animation component can generate major advances in the relevant technologies that themselves can become commercially viable as production software packages. In the value chain, all of these auxiliary businesses have been grouped into one general class of value-added activities relative to the film product, but they are not depicted as necessarily being related to one another, in the sense that value necessarily must be added to one before it can be added to another.

Value-added segments in the 'negative' stream

As illustrated in Figure 4.2, production of the actual film negative normally is considered to consist of three stages – pre-production, production and post-production. The value-added segments related to negative production can be divided by function using this scheme. P&A segments can interact with all three stages at various points. The following is a description of the segments in each stream.

Pre-production

- *Property acquisition.* A property is identified as being suitable for transformation into a film. Contracts with the property owner are negotiated, often involving up-front payment for film rights, generating an immediate additional level of value even if exploitation is not realised.
- *Project finance and distribution.* The film project is sold to investors and to studios that provide distribution. Value is added to the product in the form both of development and production capital and distribution guarantees. Currently increasing investment is raised through complex co-production arrangements and specialised financial instruments.
- *Property development.* Further value is added to the property by transposing it into a screenplay and storyboards that set out the dialogue and scene structure for the film. This stage may include selection and contracting of key creative personnel who further add intangible 'personality' value. Production and post-production schedules are drawn up.

- *Cast and crew assembly.* Actors, directors and technical crew are contracted, co-ordinated and scheduled. Creative and administrative personnel are contracted to design, realise and organise all aspects of the production.

Production

- *Production design and organisation.* This includes the design, selection, construction, acquisition and set-up of sets, properties, costumes, make-up, sound, music and special effects as well as management of filming locations.
- *Shooting.* Live action and background sequences are photographed and recorded. Most of the intangible 'personality' and 'look-and-feel' value is added by various creative professions.

Post-production

- *Processing and special effects (SFX).* The negatives are processed and any required special effects are produced and incorporated into the negative.
- *Picture editing.* Filmed segments are sequenced into a 'final cut' of the completed visual product.
- *Sound and music production and editing.* Voice-overs, sound effects and music are created, recorded and added to the negative. This represents the final level of 'creative' value-added in the negative stream.

Value-added segments in the P&A stream

- *Market research and preparation.* Often undertaken in conjunction or prior to pre-production, potential consumer interest is assessed and promotional and advertising strategies are planned.
- *Marketing, publicity and public relations.* As early as the property acquisition stage and often co-ordinated with the production and post-production stages, the film is announced, advertised and promoted.
- *Duplication.* Prints of the final, fully edited master negative are produced. Marketing and promotion functions inform the duplication function, determining duplication quantities and scheduling.
- *Distribution.* Prints are distributed to cinemas and/or to other distribution venues – including under various agreements and licenses to video rentals and sales, television exhibition and to online distributors. Marketing and

promotion functions inform the distribution function, determining locations and schedules.

Value-added segments in the exhibition stream

- *Cinema.* The cinema owner (or chain) adds value to the film by exhibiting it in locations that are convenient to potential audiences and in surroundings that are conducive to promoting film attendance – including the provision of high-technology sound and projection systems.
- *Broadcast TV.* Broadcasters add value by providing an additional outlet for the public distribution of motion pictures when they are not on cinema release.
- *Pay-TV.* Value is added either in the same way as for broadcast media, or by making analogue film products available in digital formats that allow video-on-demand access over broadband.
- *DVD and videocassette.* Value is added as analogue film products are converted into storage formats suitable for consumer rental and purchase, or for specialised distribution venues like airlines. With DVDs, further value can be added by translating analogue film products into digital formats.
- *Online distribution.* Adds similar value to video-on-demand, but also additional value in the form of (legal) downloads and links to various enhanced services – search tools, information and education sites and links to advertising and promotional materials.

Value-added segments in the auxiliary product stream

- *Advertising.* Motion pictures are used as generators of advertising revenue for products that are unrelated to the films as such. Firms pay film producers for 'product placement' in film scenes.
- *Merchandise.* Various forms of merchandise can be developed either from elements of the film itself or from the characters or story lines. From the film itself, these include the sound track and featured song CDs. In the latter category, these include toys, games, clothing and memorabilia.
- *Media spin-offs.* Films are often developed out of existing books, plays, TV series or other films, and they may also generate these spin-offs. Many films now have follow-up books or illustrated comics and some have theatrical shows (*e.g. The Lion King*). Properties can be exploited collaboratively, *e.g.* the sale of a special edition book with cover visuals from the filmed version.

- *Technology spin-offs.* Films are becoming highly technological, especially in special effects and animation. Increasingly the technological requirements of specific films spur development of new production tools and solutions. These can then become products or services that are available commercially to producers of other films.

For purposes of clarity, Figure 4.2 does not show all of the many linkages and feedbacks that exist between segments. Obvious and necessary links are shown, but the value chain contains many other essential feedback loops. For example, in the cinema markets, close communication is maintained between the exhibition and the duplication/distribution segments in order that film prints can be replaced as they wear out. But such loops exist on the commercial side also, monitoring and assessment of the performance of certain types of film products in various exhibition and auxiliary venues can feed back into producer strategies for new product development.

Differences in the value chain for different film and video products

The value chain in Figure 4.2 has been constructed with reference mainly to feature films. The basic features of the chain apply in other audio-visual product contexts, but with important variations. Short films contain much the same value-added structure as feature films although activity in many segments may be much less intense and costly for short films or non-features. Documentaries may not require actors or a range of production professionals, but likewise they may not be able to exploit a wide range of auxiliary markets.

Animated films

In the value chain as applied to animated feature films, many of which are computer generated, the main differences lie in the production technology and in various aspects of the supply chain. Otherwise, the value-added structure of *Shrek* is not much different to that of *Titanic* or any other live action/special effects hybrid. *Shrek* used human actors both for voice-overs and for purposes of motion modelling for digitally animated characters.

Figure 4.3. The production sequence of an animated film

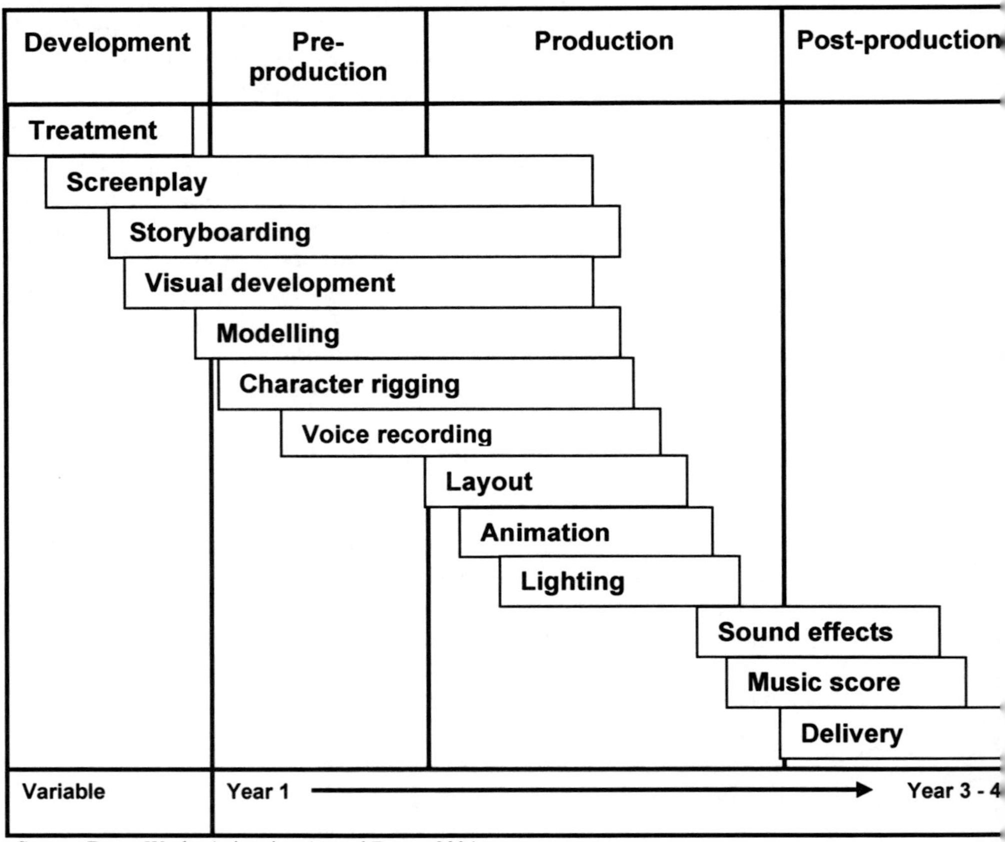

Source: DreamWorks Animation Annual Report 2004.

The production sequence for animated films (derived from DreamWorks Animation) is shown in Figure 4.3. Animated films have analogues of all of the design and technical segments of live films in roughly the same value-added sequence, except that production personnel work in computer studios rather than on sound stages and locations. The one major structural difference is that the shooting, processing and special effects segments become essentially one single production operation.

Television

Some motion picture products are made directly in the video medium, especially if intended for television or direct-to-video release. In such cases, the negative value-added stream will be found essentially to be the same for many video products (especially for entertainment products – serials, sitcoms, etc.) as for film-based productions. The technical media will be different, but the same basic value-added segments apply. In principle, the only non-applicable value-added segment is cinema release.

The most significant value chain variation overall concerns the release of original programming on broadcast television (terrestrial or cable). As illustrated in Figure 4.4, the value chain for 'stock' programming (not for 'flow' programming) differs somewhat in both the P&A and exhibition streams. For original television programming, the P&A stream is largely replaced by:

- *Programming.* Broadcasters research the market and acquire filmed programs.
- *Packaging.* Once selected, programs are allocated to channels and often bundled into programming packages. This function is performed by broadcasters in conjunction with telecommunication operators (public network and cable network operators).
- *Transmission.* Most television programs are distributed to broadcasters via public telecommunication networks. Telecommunication operators assign transmission modalities and channels and set up coding and decoding facilities.
- *Sales.* Broadcasters sell the assembled program packages to various exhibitors and sponsors.

Figure 4.4. Value chain variations in the television segment

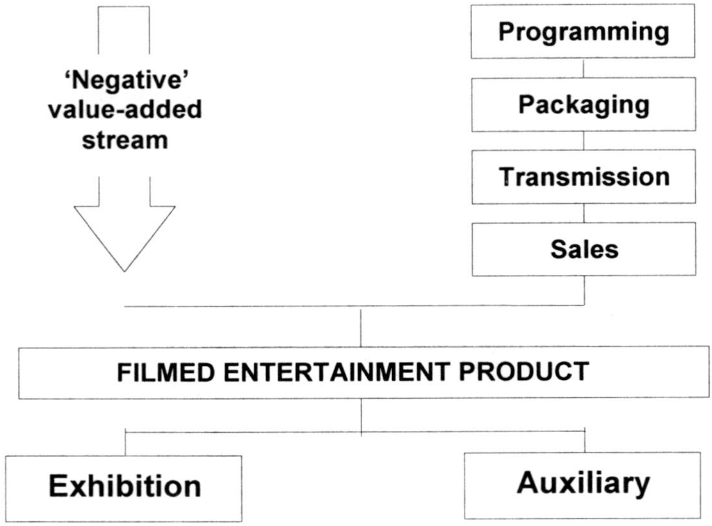

Source: Adapted from Zerdick *et al* (2000).

The primary reason for most of these variations is that the commercial model for broadcast television is different from that of cinema films in being mostly advertising-based. Revenues are earned by selling programs to advertisers, not directly to viewers. In the broadcast environment, only via DVD sell-through and merchandising do consumers pay producers directly for film and related products.

Summary

The value chain for filmed entertainment products reflects the fact that in many respects these products are not final products, but intermediate goods that support a large number of exhibition markets and further exploitation outside of the exhibition environment. Increasingly, the medium of first release – cinema, television, etc. – is not the primary source of return on investment. However, further investment is required in order to maximise revenue at every stage following completion of the core film product. Some of this investment is already fixed or sunk (*e.g.* cinema screens), but some is geared to specific products (*e.g.* games and toys).

Although there are differences between the film and video environments, the value-added structure for both cinema films and television programming is essentially the same in the negative stream and analogous in the P&A stream. Animated films likewise are very similar to live action films.

Except for more recent evolution in the exhibition and auxiliary markets, and despite very high levels of digitisation in many production and post-production segments, the value chain is largely identical to what would have applied 20-30 years ago. The effects of recent technical change (and digitisation in particular), have been more by way of generating new commercial possibilities and models rather than structural alteration in the chains. Nevertheless, further technical change may begin to challenge some parts of this structure. The ultimate challenge for the value chain may come from digital cinema, which likely will encourage the film and video media to converge even further.

Chapter 5

TECHNICAL CHANGE AND VALUE CHAIN EVOLUTION

The commercial and competitive strategies of motion picture producers are often linked to technological advances. Much of the technological infrastructure in the industry value chain is heavily digitised and the output of many segments appears entirely or partly in digital form. But different kinds of digital technologies affect different segments of the value chain in different ways and significant changes to the established value chain are likely from new digital image capture and digital distribution, with digital cinema likely to be extremely important.

This chapter focuses on digitisation in three separate but related technological environments:

- *Production technologies* relate mainly to the production and post-production segments in the 'negative' value stream. Examples include computer animation, computer-generated special effects, editing and synchronising technologies and the production elements of digital cinema.
- *Distribution technologies* relate mainly to various electronic facilities and infrastructures for delivering motion picture content to consumers. They include cable, terrestrial and satellite distribution networks (analogue and digital), telecommunication networks, Internet services, physical media (*e.g.* DVDs) and the exhibition elements of digital cinema.
- *Commercialisation technologies* relate mainly to the organisation and execution of commercial transactions related to the production or distribution of motion picture content. They include marketing and distribution platforms, electronic marketplaces and e-commerce portals.

Within each category a distinction must be drawn between *specific* technologies (mainly for production and distribution) that are developed primarily for application to film and video products and over whose development segments of the film industry have sole or substantial control, and *generic* technologies that may be relevant for film and video products but are not developed or applied in ways that differ in substance from the way they are applied in other industry contexts.

Figure 5.1 illustrates that many key segments of the value chain are fully or substantially digitised:

- In the *'negative' stream*, much of the production design and organisation is computerised (*e.g.* computer-aided design, resource management technologies). The processing and special effects segment is highly digitised (the main exception is processing analogue film) and picture editing is typically a process of analogue-digital-analogue conversion. Sound and music recording and editing are completely digital.
- In the *P&A stream* there is extensive use of Internet-based facilities to promote new productions and to gather data on consumer trends and preferences.
- In the *exhibition stream*, an increasing proportion of the television market is digitised (*i.e.* digital TV and HDTV) especially in the pay-per-view and VOD segments. Digital hard media (DVD, CD) have replaced analogue videocassettes, and online distribution is entirely digital.
- In the *auxiliary stream*, some merchandise and media spin-off segments have substantial digital components (music, computer games, etc.) and technology spin-offs (*e.g.* production technologies) typically are entirely digital.

Some of the segments in the value chain have no particularly special technological characteristics or dependencies. The pre-production segments, for example, are primarily about doing business deals. However, as will be shown further below, technological developments in other segments may be shaping some of these pre-production functions as well.

Variations in digitisation characteristics can be found for some types of television products and for animated films where digital image capture already has largely displaced film-based cinematography. For many programs made expressly for television, the shooting segment is now digitised also, utilising mainly tape-based digital video recording technology. Digital broadcasting technology has fully digitised the distribution of broadcast programming in markets where such services are available. For animated films, virtually the entire process is digitised in the television environment and all segments except duplication and distribution are digitised in the cinema segment.

Figure 5.1. Existing digitisation in value chain segments

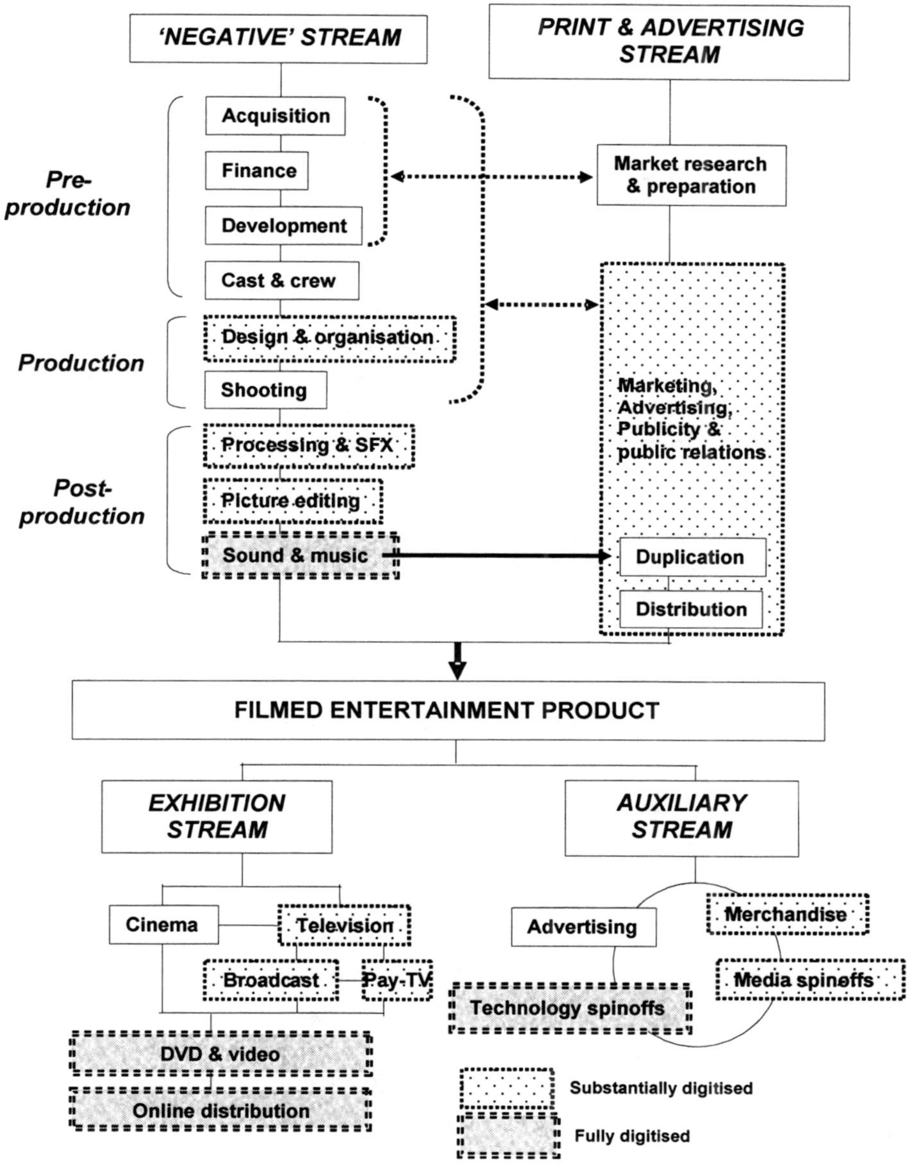

Overall, however, even though the basic value chain has seen progressive digitisation in most segments where this offers obvious advantages, the basic value-added structure of the chain has not changed substantively in 30-40 years. Digitisation appears to have resulted in technological substitution and the expansion of business opportunities, particularly in the post-production and exhibition streams, rather than in major alteration in the basic value-added structure. Digital recording, animation, special effects, DVD, VOD, addressable cable networks, etc. will continue to generate new opportunities and revenues for producers, distributors and network operators, but they have not yet had a major effect upon the structure of the value chain.

At the present time, the most significant technological evolution in the production environment is occurring in segments that until recently have been relatively untouched by digitisation. In the cinema environment specifically, this concerns mainly the shooting, duplication and distribution segments (Zhu 2001; Silver and Alpert 2003; Currah 2003; Husak 2004; Altman *et al.* 2006). Most motion pictures, whether intended for cinema or television release, are still shot on film. As such, these segments together constitute the principal remaining bottleneck in the complete digitisation of the value chain. The arrival of digital cinema may challenge this, and may be the single most significant new stimulus to value chain evolution.

Full digitisation of the value chain

Until comparatively recently, both cinema and television production used analogue imaging technologies – some of them film-based and others tape-based. Analogue video recording has been a staple television technology since the 1960s, but its application has been limited to specific types of programs – *e.g.* it was generally not used for prime-time dramatic programming. Thus, most prime-time television features have been shot on film in exactly the same way as cinema features. Since the 1990s, both film and video media have been exploring and adopting various digital production and exhibition technologies, but not always the same technologies.

The television environment is now moving decisively to digital imaging and digital program delivery in both broadcast and pay-per-view modes. Conversion to digital television is facilitated in that much of the capital cost of conversion is contributed by consumers in the form of new television receivers, set-top boxes, satellite dishes, home entertainment centres, etc. Converting the cinema environment is far more complex and adoption of digital cinema far less advanced. However, as shown in Figure 3.3 the growth in digital cinema screens is rapid even though they represent only a fraction of total capacity (no more than 1% of screens in OECD countries). If this transition accelerates, this is likely to have major effects upon the shooting, duplication, distribution and exhibition segments of the value chain.

Digital cinema promises to add value for all stakeholders. Cinema audiences are offered an enhanced viewing experience that could increase box office sales. Cinema operators and distributors will have to absorb significant conversion costs, but in return they may obtain greater flexibility in allocating screen capacity and increasing access to new types of cinema products and packages. Full conversion to digital cinema would result in the complete digitisation of the production and exhibition streams, and further narrow the technological distinctions between film and television markets. At the production level, it is likely that digital cinema eventually would facilitate more economical transfer of products between film and television markets.

Cinema film producers stand to benefit most from reduced duplication and distribution costs. A feature film of about two hours consists of six projection reels, each weighing approximately 40 kg. Duplication costs per film are USD 750-1200, depending on the number of prints (setting up the duplication process forms a major part of these costs so costs per reel vary with the quantity of prints produced). Moreover, prints have an extremely limited life span; they deteriorate in proportion to the number of times they are projected (Husak 2004). It has been estimated that eliminating duplication and distribution costs could save distributors worldwide over USD 2 billion annually (Fritz 2005).

If digital cinema increases image quality and lowers *production* as well as *distribution* costs, there are clear implications for industry structure. Historically, film-based production costs have been considered high enough to constitute barriers to market entry. If the costs for cinema-quality digital production decline significantly below film-based costs these barriers may be reduced. However, owing to the labour-intensive nature of film production, there is no guarantee that costs will fall, especially in the short to medium term (more about this in Chapter 6). Although digital cinema is designed for the professional production environment, it is intriguing to speculate that some variant of this technology may eventually spill over into consumer markets in the same way as other high-end professional technologies have done (*e.g.* video recording, digital sound recording and digital photography). The wider availability of cinema-quality or near cinema-quality production technology may encourage an increase in independent small-scale productions.

What is digital cinema?

Digital cinema uses digital images processed with software to replace chemically produced images on plastic film. Digital cinema images can be generated or captured entirely in digital form, or created through the combination of analogue and digital images (*e.g.* digital scanning of analogue film). The main differences between new digital *cinematography* systems and various existing digital *video* systems concern image quality. Digital cinema produces images that are denser (more pixels), deeper (more bits per pixel) and that utilise a much greater colour spectrum. Owing to these differences, digital cinema compression systems must be flexible with regard both to channel capacity and storage. This flexibility allows for much higher image resolution than conventional video, such that the projected digital image is comparable to a film image, but without the attendant mechanical degradation.

In existing video systems the input signal is compressed into a bit rate that is limited by a fixed channel capacity. Image sequence coding schemes that have been standardised internationally include MPEG-1 for digital video at 2 megabits per second, MPEG-2 for television broadcasting at 10 Mbps, H.261 for videoconferencing at 64 kilobits per second and H.263 at very low bit rates (below 20 Kbps). The bandwidth for digital television currently is limited at 19.39 Mbps and DVD is limited to approximately 9 gigabytes of total data at a 10 Mbps data rate. Video recording has always been a trade-off between the available bit rate and image quality; a reduction in bit rate generally giving lower decoded image quality.

The current digital production environment for television includes two resolution thresholds – standard definition (SD) that is sufficient for most television 'flow' programming or for some types of short programs, and high-definition (HD) that is preferred for features, especially where cinematographic quality is essential to the look-and-feel of the product (*e.g.* nature and wildlife programs). But digital cinema requires much higher resolution than HDTV. Television is viewed typically at distances that are three times the height of the picture. Cinema audiences view films at 1 to 1.5 times the picture height. The greater the picture height, the greater must be the resolution.

The basic digital cinema architecture consists of a storage facility to which the digital content is transferred and a decoding facility to project the film optically onto a conventional cinema screen. Eventually, motion picture files could be distributed to exhibitors via satellite or fibre-optic links on digital telecommunication networks, very similar to transmitting broadcast television programs. The files can be either stored by exhibitors on local servers or there can be continuous relay via optical fibre connections. In practice, however, the current costs of such transmissions are too high. For the present, most digital cinema productions are delivered to exhibitors in hard media (usually on high-capacity external hard discs).

Initial take-up of digital cinema technology (which includes encoding and decoding software, file servers and special projectors) was slow due to lack of industry-wide standards (Perry 2005). In March 2002, Disney, Fox, MGM, Paramount, Sony Pictures Entertainment, Universal and Warner Bros. Studios created the Digital Cinema Initiative (DCI) joint venture, to "establish and document specifications for an open architecture for Digital Cinema that ensures a uniform and high level of technical performance, reliability, and quality control" (DCI 2005). DCI was established to develop technical specifications and also to shape these specifications such that they reflected the business interests of the consortium (Husak 2004). Currently, the DCI specifications cover three main areas:

- *File formats and exchange.* Basically, digital cinema specifications are modelled on the workflow of analogue film production. Digital Cinema Distribution Master (DCDM) data file formats provide an interchange standard so that digital cinema files can be transferred between production and post-production segments in any facility that adheres to the standard. A DCDM is extracted from a Digital Source Master (DSM) – which is an assembly of all of the post-production components that make up a finished motion picture – and can then be passed between the various stages of production. The completed DCDM files are then assembled into a Digital Cinema Package (DCP) for distribution to cinemas. The DCP also can be sent directly to post-production quality control systems. The DCDM requires standardised file formats for all the constituent motion picture elements. Thus, the DCDM will contain DCI-developed specifications for image, audio, subtitle and auxiliary data. Each file within the DCDM carries information to support frame-based synchronization with other files (DCI 2005).
- *Packaging.* These standards concern the storage of digital cinema content and its transmission to the site where it will be decoded for viewing. Since there may be multiple sources of content, a common interchange standard for digital cinema between post-production and exhibition is required. For the Digital Cinema Package (DCP), DCI specified the use of existing MXF and XML conformant files for packaging the DCDM (image, audio and subtitle) files.
- *Transportation.* The major studios identified digitised transport as the major area for cost savings. Digital content can be transported to projection sites using physical media (*e.g.* hard discs), virtual private networks or satellite communications. A key DCI concern is security

and robustness of the files; the content owner's encryption may not be removed during transport, thus preserving content security.

Digital cinema and the value chain

The digital cinema architecture is based on the existing value chain, and the DCI digital cinema model is more or less the digital equivalent of the long-established analogue film production model. Instead of clips of film being assembled mechanically into 'dailies' (or 'rushes') and then into rough and finished cuts, the clips, rushes and cuts become digitally stored sequences in standardised file and transport formats.

However, the sequence and speed with which files are processed and manipulated in the post-production system may act to truncate the value chain. Digital techniques in widespread use in post-production include non-linear-non-destructive editing, 3D compositing and digital colour grading. Most post-production companies can digitise a film in real time to 2k resolution with 8-bit colour depth. Film scanning technology will enable greater resolution and colour depth (4k and 12 bit respectively). Sony's Grating Light Valve display technology is believed to be capable of supporting 8k resolution. With digital cinema it is possible in principle to merge elements of shooting, processing, SFX and editing so that each completed portion of the film could be evaluated in cinema-ready form right from the very first takes. However, the actual value-added structure would not necessarily change for various production and post-production service providers, even though they may work on tighter, more closely integrated schedules.

Developing the digital cinema market

The final and most challenging step in introducing digital cinema is to equip exhibitors with the technology. There are at least 70 000 cinema screens in the OECD area and current conversion cost estimates are USD 75 000-100 000 per screen (Husak 2004). This represents at least a USD 5.5 billion *new* market for digital cinema exhibition systems even before any additional markets emerge for new digital production technologies.

This costly process may well involve both private and public sector interests. With digital *television* in the UK, for example, the public broadcaster helped bridge the conversion gap by imposing an orderly schedule and making digital broadcast signals available terrestrially at nominal cost by means of one-payment set-top boxes. Similar kinds of actions may be forthcoming from public agencies regarding digital cinema. In the UK, for example, the British Film Council, a government agency that promotes the film and video industries, has instituted a fund to bring digital projection to

240 screens, thus accelerating the schedule for digital conversion (*Financial Times* 2007).

Nevertheless, a significant grouping of companies also has formed to develop and distribute digital cinema technology. Most immediately, companies are now developing new and improved digital projectors that are compliant with JPEG 2000 image compression specifications. They are also developing alternative techniques for image compression, for coding/decoding and for transportation of digital files to exhibition sites through satellite communication and fibre-optic networks. Table 5.1 lists firms that currently appear to be in the forefront of developing, marketing, adopting and distributing various digital cinema elements. Companies that distribute digital content (including digital movies, advertising for digital screens and live-event streaming) from production sites to exhibition sites include Dolby Digital, CineMedia, DFE Technologies and Access Integrated Technologies Inc.

Table 5.1. Firms active in the development of digital cinema technologies

Production	Post-production	Software	Transportation/ distribution	Exhibition
Analog Devices	Imagica	Access Integrated Technologies Inc.	Access Integrated Technologies Inc.	Kinepolis
Barco	Industrial Light & Magic	Adobe	CineMedia (Regal Entertainment)	Landmark Theatres
Christie	LaserPacific Media Corporation	Corel	DFE Technologies	Regal Entertainment
NEC	Pixar Animation Studios	Paint Shop Pro	Dolby Digital	
Sony	Technicolor			
Texas Instruments				

Business models for conversion to digital cinema

Various companies are pursuing business models where new digital equipment is provided to distributors at a subsidised cost. Christie Digital Systems (who make digital projectors) and Access Integrated Technology (who provide software and digital cinema services) plan to bring digital cinema to 2 500 screens in the US. Christie will provide equipment and maintenance, while Access Integrated Technology will provide more than USD 100 million in conversion funding. Under this scheme, distributors will receive the equipment at no cost, but will pay a 'virtual print' fee changed on a per-film basis. Another model is being pursued by Avica Technology, an Irish digital services company that is attempting to create the world's first national digital network in more than 515 cinemas. Initial investment will be recouped through savings from lower duplication costs.

As business models like these begin to appear, complementary technological strategies emerge. For example, various encoding devices are under development, which include DCI-mandated compression and encryption techniques. The decoder technology will be embedded into the digital projectors, which is cheaper but also exerts proprietary control over the algorithms.

Technological competition to increase or differentiate product qualities is also taking place. DCI has selected JPEG 2000 as the core specification for image compression because it offers a layering capability that provides flexibility to digital projectors to embed both 2k and 4k signals. This provides both equipment manufacturers and production studios with a choice of resolution. Dolby Digital has announced their own digital cinema system for managing and distributing digital films to digital projectors, indicating that within the current standards framework, competitive systems may emerge.

Exhibitors are also exploring new strategies. For example, the Belgian Kinepolis group has outfitted 21 of its screens with digital projectors, enabling them to show digitally produced blockbusters, and also alternative content. This has included a children's film that normally would have gone straight to DVD, cinema screening of a popular Belgian TV drama before it was broadcast, the screening of live-eye operations before an audience of surgeons, various live sporting events and business presentations.

In the US, Landmark Theatres are converting 210 of their cinema screens to new 4K digital SXRD projectors from Sony Electronics. This will increase their capability to show alternative content as Kinepolis has done, but the company's strategy is also to produce and distribute high-definition films. The Regal Entertainment Group (another US cinema chain) has installed Christie L6 2k digital projectors and invested approximately USD 75 million to set up a digital supply chain. To further diversify their approach, Regal has been involved in other types of digital transmissions; for example, broadcasting the Musicology tour program by the singer Prince to Regal cinemas across the US via satellite.

The proliferation of alternative content may also be aided by the strategies of some of the imaging software vendors. Adobe and Corel, for example, now offer relatively inexpensive DCI-compatible imaging tools. Competitive packages like Photoshop, Corel Draw or Paint Pro Shop now can be applied inexpensively to film products, making them attractive to lower budget independent producers.

Piracy is expected to become more of a problem with digital cinema in that the critical release window (the first weekend) will no longer be protected by issuing the product in a medium (namely film) that was more difficult to steal than a digital file and much more costly to reproduce in high quality form. End-to-end digital production offers more opportunity for content to be illegally appropriated in whole or in part before or during the critical release window. DCI specified an encryption method whereby studios compress and encode files using authentication watermarks that allow only the authorised key holder to decode the files. In addition to encryption, however, Boeing has patented a method to guard against theft of digital cinema receivers that involves embedding a GPS locator directly into the receiver itself.

Finally, in addition to all of the activities noted above, the major studios also have developed conversion strategies. Sony Pictures Entertainment has contracted Ascent Media Group, a distribution and services company, to convert the studio's extensive film, television, and other media assets into digital format, and both Universal Pictures and Walt Disney are establishing a digital production format. These three major studios have a collaborative effort to establish a USD 3 billion fund that will provide up to USD 80 000 per screening room for digital conversion at exhibition sites. The strategy is to be a first mover in establishing a complete digital supply chain, where access could be sold to other studios.

Overall, both co-operation and competition is emerging between various business segments in the production, distribution and technology sectors. All support a degree of standardisation that will lower unavoidable common costs. Technological competition is emerging among the various technology suppliers, some of whom have established markets while others are relative newcomers or are moving from peripheral to central market segments. Exhibitors are using the possibilities of digital cinema to expand their range of content options beyond what is distributed by major studios. Standardised software is also under development which will be crucial for encouraging independent producers to adopt the digital cinema production environment.

Creating new digital distribution markets for film and video products

The direct downloading of digital content is widely considered to be the most important technical change currently confronting the film and video industries. Nevertheless, particularly in the short term, online distribution continues to face competition from DVD sales and rentals and more particularly from high quality premium cable television services – especially video-on-demand. Downloading is oriented primarily to the PC environment and a typical feature film download over an ASDL link can take up to one hour, and often much longer. This is less a problem where the consumer purchases the content outright – *i.e.* acquires multi-play rights – or where DVD burning is a feature, but less attractive where single-play agreements apply.

Moreover, the network dynamics of the Internet portend much more than simple access to film and video products on downloading sites. The growth of peer-to-peer technologies like BitTorrent or Joost has become enormously significant in this context. Also, the visibility of so-called 'social networks' is escalating rapidly. These interactive audio-visual environments – oriented to uploading as well as downloading – show signs already of transforming many key aspects of how film productions are conceptualised, packaged and marketed.

Developing the online video marketplace

Currently, many online markets are devoted mostly to cinema and television content that has been produced in an analogue environment and converted to digital form for distribution. One of the most common distribution models is simple e-commerce; selling or renting DVDs online (see Chapter 2). This section analyses the more dynamic segments of online distribution that involve file downloading and/or uploading. In this report only the legitimate market is analysed; counterfeiting and piracy issues are being dealt with separately in other OECD studies (see OECD 2007a). However, IPR issues are especially problematic in the online environment. A recent report for the European Union reflects widespread industry concerns that inability to address the counterfeiting and piracy issues is leading to business decisions not to put digital content online (European Union 2006).

Although video downloading came first to public attention mostly in connection with file sharing in illegal peer-to-peer environments, the major television and film producers moved to integrate online distribution into their already extensive film and video supply chains rather more quickly than did producers in the music industry. As the President of Fox Digital Media said recently, "Our goal is to seek out as many viable retail outlets as we can, and put as many titles as we can on those sites" (OR13). Nevertheless, many doubts remain as to the viability of current distribution and pricing models, which as yet appear to offer no clear advantages over existing DVD and television distribution models.

Table 5.2 gives an indication of the current extent of legal downloading undertakings within the OECD area. Most are operated by communication and media companies, including wired and mobile telecommunication network operators as well as broadcasting networks, cable TV companies,

Table 5.2. Video download services in major OECD and neighbouring markets

Country/region	Service provider		
Austria	Telekom Austria (WWW.AON.TV)		
Australia	Telstra (BigPond Movies)		
Belgium (Flemish speaking)	Chellomedia		
Belgium (French speaking)	Chellomedia		
Benelux	Keeno		
Canada	Archambault Cogeco CTV Inc.	JumpTV Movielink MTS Rogers Sasktel	Shaw VOD Telus Videotron
Croatia	T-Croatia (T-Online)		
France	FNAC France Telecom (24/24) France Telecom (Orange TV) Free (Iliad)	Glowria Moviesystem Neuf Cegetel TF1	
Germany	In2Movies Premiere (Direkt+) Prosieben (Maxdome) T-Online (T-Vision)		
Hong Kong, China	VideOline		
Iceland	Simmin		
Italy	Eutalia Telecom Italia (Alice Home TV) Telecom Italia (Rosso Alice)		
Japan	BB Cable Cinema Cruise Cinema Now Itochu	Jupiter Cable NEO Index NTT Plala PPV Japan/K Opticom	
Korea	IMBC		
Netherlands	Chellomedia Free Record Shop Mine TV (KPN)		
Nordic (Sweden, Norway, Denmark, Finland)	Digital Distribution (Film2Home) Lyse Tele (Lyse)	Phonofile SF Anytime	
Pan-Asian	Anytime		
Spain	Telefonica (Imagenio)		
Switzerland/Liechtenstein	Teleclub (Swisscom)		
United Kingdom	Arts Alliance Arts Alliance + AOL British Telecom (BT Vision)	Home Choice (VNL) ODG/NTL (Film Flex) Wippit	
United States	Amazon Unbox AOL Apple iTunes Store BitTorrent CinemaNow	GUBA Movielink WalMart	

manufacturers of computer devices, general distributors of 'conventional' media content and entrepreneurial start-ups. In general most of these sites are aimed at specific national markets or at selected groups of countries (such as the US and Canada, or the Nordic countries). As yet, fully international markets have not emerged.

There is a significant and growing presence in this market of non-media companies and general retailers that are exploiting or planning to exploit their established brand names. For example, Wal-Mart has launched a video download service in conjunction with Comcast, the major US cable network operator that is now a part owner of MGM. Likewise, UK retailer Tesco may soon begin distributing films online, building on a track record as an e-commerce pioneer in its existing food, general merchandise and services sectors (already Tesco distributes music downloads). In addition, AT&T has launched AT&T Homezone, a new service that combines satellite TV programming, a fully featured DVR, caller-ID on TV, movies-on-demand, photo-sharing and music.

Other potential new entrants include companies that already are major distributors of DVDs. Currently the DVD rental firm Blockbuster confines its activities to e-commerce (online rentals), but there have been reports that the company is planning to launch a downloading service as well (OR13). The Amazon Unbox digital video download service was launched in September 2006 as an addition to Amazon's DVD sales business, offering television programs, cinema films and other videos.

Google entered the online video market originally via its marketing and advertising business but subsequently negotiated various agreements with content owners to offer cable TV-style distribution on the Internet. Yahoo, Google's main competitor in the browser market, has a similar plan. Microsoft will soon introduce a music/video player, but has delayed the launch of its video store until early 2007 (OR13).

As collaborative and joint ventures emerge, there may be changes in established distribution models. For example, the cable channel ESPN is collaborating with Verizon and Charter, who have interests in both television and Internet undertakings, to provide the ESPN360 radio service exclusively on these networks. The example suggests that major cable services and ISPs may elect make exclusive arrangements with specific content providers to show some types of content only through specific networks (OR12). This runs counter to the currently established practice of distributing content across different cable networks.

Several new initiatives suggest possible directions in which online distribution might go. Following on from its highly successful iTunes initiative, Apple is launching video downloads on its iTunes site, integrated with its video iPods. In this case, Apple had initial difficulty negotiating with the studios due to its insistence on a single price for all film downloads. Apple offered the studios USD 14 per film with the intention of selling all of them online for a flat rate of USD 14.99. Microsoft and Sony are working on a competitive device-based download environment, and the digital music service Napster likewise is moving into films and video games, using its existing user network (OR13).

At present, all of these undertakings, actual and planned, are oriented to four basic distribution models. Three are 'one-to-one' downloads whereby content is transferred directly from the publisher:

- *On-demand streaming (S).* Content is divided into many small segments and downloaded and buffered to the user's computer sequentially, or out-of-order, allowing users to fast forward and rewind.
- *On-demand downloading (D).* Content is transferred in a single large segment with no out-of-order downloading or viewing.
- *Download and burn (B).* Content must be downloaded and recorded to a standard writable optical disc by the user.

The remaining model creates a 'many-to-many' environment:

- *Peer-to-peer downloading and streaming (P).* Content is transferred via a public peer-to-peer network based for example on the BitTorrent data transfer protocol (in use by companies such as BitTorrent, Inc. which uses a rental download model) and being developed for Joost (created by Baaima, N.V., who are developing a TV-quality peer-to-peer platform for streaming video programs, supported by advertising), or from a controlled, private peer-to-peer network such as Verisign's Kontiki.

BitTorrent and other peer-to-peer file distribution protocols allow consumers also to become distributors of the same content. By offloading a large part of content distribution to users, the peer-to-peer distribution method reduces upstream bandwidth requirements for the publisher (with the additional requirement, however, of a substantial base of on-line subscribers to help redistribute the content). Despite the potential distribution cost savings, peer-to-peer distribution of licensed on-line content has yet to gain significant traction (Kontiki being a slight exception).

BitTorrent, Inc. remains the peer-to-peer technology leader, but has only just begun to provide a significant number of licensed movie downloads via a commercial service despite signing an agreement with Warner Bros. Entertainment Group to do so in 2006 (Warner serves the German market through an agreement with In2Movies, using a different peer-to-peer protocol). However BitTorrent Entertainment Network was launched end-

February 2007 and the new service has reported compiling rights to more than 3 000 movies, 1 000 games and 1 000 music videos from 34 participating content providers (Reuters 2007). Publishers may use DRM in all distribution methods to restrict playback abilities, but peer-to-peer distribution requires strong digital rights management technologies to prevent unintended sharing of content files with unauthorised users.[12]

Table 5.3 lists some of the advantages and disadvantages of each downloading environment along with examples of well-known service providers in each environment. Although most legal downloading occurs in one of the three 'one-to-one' environments outlined above, quite clearly there is as yet no single environment that is optimal for all types of consumers in all types of situations. Moreover, each provider offers a different range and quantity of titles. Thus, the consumer may encounter situations where the desired title is not available in a downloading environment that suits a particular consumption context. For example, on-demand streaming may be immediate, but maybe not transferable to a television receiver or to a wide-screen home entertainment system, limiting its appeal largely to individual viewing.

Competing with DVDs and television

Given that the downloading environment is not commercially or technologically homogenous and that its efficiency is partly dependent on bandwidth availability, the obvious question concerns how competitive this model will be vis-à-vis DVDs and premium cable TV services, or with new global TV services such as Joost. Two key issues are *1)* the business and pricing models and *2)* the consumption characteristics of the technological environment. The challenge for online distribution will be not just to attract consumers, but to increase consumer *retention* and to develop a consumer preference for direct downloading. This likely will entail creating a simpler, better co-ordinated and more user friendly downloading environment.

12. Using one of several BitTorrent software applications, a publisher generates and distributes a small '.torrent' file via web sites, e-mail, physical media or some other means to 'peers' who wish to have a copy of the original content. Peers run the BitTorrent software with the .torrent file provided by the publisher to receive the original content from the publisher's computer in small pieces which are assembled automatically once all of the pieces have arrived. Each peer downloads all the pieces of the content in a different order, subject to the availability of desired pieces among seeders and peers, provided that each peer has a different (and growing) set of pieces of the original content. Since peers also download missing pieces from each other, many effective copies (sources) of the content may be available to a downloader at any one time, even though the original publisher only released one copy and even if no peer has an entire copy. When each peer has received an entire copy of the original content, the user may decide to continue to seed the torrent, uploading the content to others like the original publisher, or to disconnect the torrent. Other peer-to-peer protocols operate in a similar manner.

Table 5.3. Comparison of on-line motion picture delivery technologies

Delivery method	Advantages	Disadvantages	Bandwidth requirements	Examples
On-demand streaming	Viewable immediately	Content not generally portable to other devices	High: Delays degrade viewing experience, must be downloaded in real time or better	Google Video, CinemaNow
On-demand download	Content sometimes transferable to non-PC playback devices	Content was not viewable until entirely downloaded; newer technology allows viewing from time downloading starts	Moderate: Content can arrive as network conditions permit, not in real time	Apple iPod, iTunes and Apple TV
Download and burn	Viewable on PC and any DVD player	User must create DVD	High: Large files required for DVD resolution	CinemaNow
Peer-to-peer (private and public)	Infrastructure build-out not required, performance generally increases with more users	No Quality of Service, requires critical mass of peers, little control over distribution geography	Low for publishers: Users pay for redistribution High for users: As much as 40% transmission overhead	BitTorrent protocol, Kontiki; Publishers: TUVnetworks (China), Joost (created byBaaima, N.V.)

Regarding business model and pricing issues, downloading must compete with the already very large market for DVDs and the increased availability of flexible high-definition pay-per-view digital cable facilities and new advertisement-based TV services such as Joost. As shown in Chapter 2, the DVD market has grown much faster over a much shorter period than the videocassette market. Moreover, the DVD delivers a substantial quality increment over the videocassette, which, when added to concomitant improvements in home entertainment technologies, is making home viewing a much more generally attractive option. Premium cable TV services have the immediate advantage of being integrated already into the high-quality home audio-visual device market. At this point, only some of the downloading environments offer easy or dependable linkage to the installed base of home entertainment devices.

Table 5.4. Pricing and service models of a selection of legal download sites (prices in USD)

Provider	Cost	S	D	B	P	Service
Amazon Unbox	TV: $2/episode (own); movies: $3-4 (rental), $10-15 (own)	♦	♦	♦		>650 TV series, > 3000 films. Can burn to DVD, and transfer to WMP media devices
Apple iTunes Store	TV: $2/episode Movies: $10-15 Shorts: $2	♦	♦			200 TV shows, >260 films, 155 shorts
BitTorrent, Inc.	Free		♦	♦	♦	No recent commercial offerings. Approx 30 pre-1950s movies free at BitTorrent.com.
CinemaNow (US)	Subscription: $29.95/month, $99.95/year; individual purchase: $9.99	♦	♦			1 500 movies available, for viewing on PC only
GUBA (US)	24-hour rental: $3-4 (movies), $1.79 (TV episodes); purchase: $10-30 (movies)	♦	♦			Approximately 600 movies and TV series available
JumpTV (Canada)	Each channel or package: $10-25/month	♦				Over 200 live ethnic TV channels and film packages
Movielink (US)	Purchase: $10-20; rent: $1.19-4.00	♦	♦			Accessible from the US only
Moviesystem (France)	$1.95-6.55 per view/per film	♦	♦	♦		Online platform for Canal Plus VOD - approximately 110 titles available
TVUnNetwork	Free	♦			♦	Several dozen TV channels from around the world
Wal-Mart	TV: $2/episode Movies: $7.50-14.88	♦	♦			>1 000 movies, >60 TV series. May be downloaded to portables
Wippit (UK)	Purchase: $11-43	♦	♦			Approximately 100 films available

Notes:

1. Where DVD recording is indicated, the table indicates only distributors that offer recording as a service optio Many downloaded movies for which 'burn' privileges are not granted can be recorded illegally using third-part software.

2. BitTorrent, Inc. distributes files in several downloadable file formats, including files intended to be recorded t DVD. Although the BitTorrent protocol does not support streaming explicitly, the ability to view files whe downloading (effectively streaming) depends on file format contained in the torrent, and the media player used b the downloading party.

3. Purchases are often limited to the home markets. The US sites all appear accessible to Canadian customers excep Movielink. In general most of these sites are aimed at specific national markets or at selected groups of countrie such as the US and Canada, the Nordic countries, etc.

At present, no reliable comparative industry-wide data on download pricing is available. However, the currently operational commercial download sites appear to be settling upon a somewhat consistent set of service and pricing models (some sites offering a blend of models). Table 5.4 lists the models and published prices from a group of legal download sites, selected from Table 5.2. The group covers several national markets in the OECD region and also a range of different service types, from distribution of mainline cinema and television content to specialist audio-visual content.

With few exceptions, the range of service models and prices observed in the 11 companies described in Table 5.4 (see descriptions above of 'S', 'D', 'B', 'P' in table heading) were replicated in various forms and combinations in the other download sites. Prices for individual films and for content packages (subscriptions) varied over the period in which this review was compiled. In many cases prices are rather fluid as providers search for the right price/service level. The current business models can be summarised as follows:

- *Rental downloads.* This model is an analogue of the conventional DVD rental. The difference is that the film or TV program is downloaded rather than ordered as a rental DVD. The consumer obtains the right to download a film or television program for a specified period of time (typically 24 hours). Most services allow for the download to be viewed multiple times during the rental period. The files remain on the PC, but they contain DRM that disables playback beyond the agreed rental period.

  Prices for these services in the sample group ranged between USD 1 and USD 4, usually determined by the nature or release date of the product (new releases normally pushing the top end of the price scale). Download rentals are on average comparable or cheaper than DVD rentals, but the period of use (usually 24 hours) is much less. Many DVD rental firms now offer up to 30 days possession with unlimited plays for under USD 6.

- *Purchase downloads.* This model is an analogue of the established DVD sell-through model, whether through conventional or e-commerce retail outlets. The difference is only that the content is delivered on-line. Two transfer modalities can be applied:

  – *Download purchase to a PC hard disc or a portable media player*: The DRM attached to the video file will tie the content to a particular computer or media player. Content may be viewed any number of times on this device, but the file is not transferable to any other device. However, in some cases the device may be connected legally to a television monitor.

  - *Download purchase to a DVD*: Often referred to as 'burning', this model allows content to be downloaded and recorded onto a DVD. The model has advantages for the user in that the DVD may then be played on any number of devices, but disadvantages for the publisher in that more consumers can have access to the same download on different devices.

  Unlike rental downloads, the range of prices for online purchases is wide – *ca.* USD 10 to *ca.* USD 40 – varying significantly according to the type of product and the country in which the distributor was based. For the largest distributors with the most extensive catalogues, an average price of about USD 10 is applied to most products. Generally, prices in this segment are comparable to or even slightly cheaper than offline forms of distribution. The main disadvantage for the consumer is that most of the legal download sites restrict the portability of content.

- *Subscription downloads*. This model allows consumers to access a range of titles on a monthly or yearly basis for a single subscription fee. The model is not entirely unique, but it does provide a different type of environment in which consumers can access a variety of content for a relatively small fee.

  Prices vary according to the package, but CinemaNow (one of the largest online distributors) has set its prices at USD 29.99 for a monthly subscription and USD 99.99 for a yearly subscription. Depending upon frequency of use, these prices may represent a considerable bargain over DVD and cable. They represent the one identified example of aggressive online pricing and service packaging.

It would appear overall that apart from the issue of rental periods and content portability, downloads are now basically competitive in price both with offline distribution methods and with e-commerce DVD rentals and sales. That the online download market has not yet dominated the distribution markets altogether clearly is not a consequence of price.

However, there remain many technical and 'look-and-feel' issues that likely will require online distributors to create a technical interface with the home exhibition environment that is at least comparable or maybe superior to those offered by DVD and cable TV. The main remaining advantage to DVD and VoD would appear to be that their markets are very well co-ordinated technologically. All DVD sell-through or rental products and all cable services work reliably on most of the installed base of consumer equipment without special set-ups or PC connections. Most products are backward and forward compatible. Although several of the major online download services now provide an interface with the enhanced home entertainment environment, the process is never as straightforward as playing a DVD or making a VoD selection. The device-based strategies of Apple and perhaps eventually Microsoft and Sony are possible solutions, but there are other co-ordination issues as well.

Overall, online distributors continue to face many technical challenges, including:

- Lack of and/or inconsistency in the availability fast Internet connections.
- Software incompatibilities.
- Unreliability of high-quality video streaming.
- Audio detection problems (sound card software in one region might not work in another region).
- Lack of optimum techniques for high quality downloading to a computer hard-drive or to DVD.
- Lack of standardisation for distribution platforms.

Some of these challenges are beyond the control of distributors; for example, network speed depends on both the network provider and the consumer. Moreover, as the consumer pays more for high-bandwidth Internet connections, expectations regarding video download quality increase. Thus, the vendor has to implement more expensive compression techniques to ensure high product and service quality.

On the standardisation front, the simultaneous availability of different video file formats, encoding and compression techniques creates confusion for vendors and consumers. Content can be produced using established products like Windows Media, QuickTime and Real, or they may employ improved techniques, for example, .avi, or .divx. However, not every consumer will have the technical capability to reconfigure their computers for each new environment. For the online market to compete, vendors will have to be able to provide content that works with the set-up that the consumer already possesses.

To sum up, the key issue for online distribution is not just customer attraction but also consumer *retention,* which means that the overall co-ordination of the online download environment will have to improve. But important as downloading is likely to become as a new source of revenue from digital content, so far there are no clear indications that downloading of conventional film and video content as such will result in significant change to the structure of the value chain. These download markets may increase in size, but other models of interaction with audio-visual content on the Internet suggest potentially much more significant changes in the characteristics of these products and in the relationships between producers and consumers.

Social networks and online markets

The 'social network' is one of the most interesting recent developments in online film and video distribution. Websites such as YouTube and MySpace, although oriented to the exhibition of content produced by consumers, also provide commercial film and video distributors with a very different venue for their products, and this aspect has become increasingly important in the commercial development of these sites. Social network sites have special characteristics and a level of popularity that indicate an increasingly significant role for them in the digital content marketplace (see OECD 2007c, a study specifically on user-created content).

Social Internet networks began life as providers of facilities whereby anyone could upload personal video files at no cost to share them with other website users. However, although the websites provided the basic facility for distributing this content, users could form their own subnetworks spontaneously based upon their interest in various types of content. Site operators have set ground rules regarding copyrighted images and objectionable content and generally they filter out objectionable or offensive material, but otherwise the dynamics of these sub-networks are determined largely by the preferences and behaviours of users.

The important initial difference between social networks and the commercial online distribution networks is that social networks were oriented originally to *uploads* – putting digital content onto the network – rather than to earning revenue from downloads or video streaming. In the beginning, the commercial and financial rationales for setting up and operating these networks were not obvious. However, some social networks have come a long way towards defining new markets that are structured around the online distribution of video files. Arguably, because of their interactive capabilities, social networks have been more successful at creating innovative market dynamics than have the conventional video download sites, which is reflected in their currently escalating market values (see OECD 2007c).

Commercial providers of downloading services such as Apple and Napster are quasi-precedents for the social video network phenomenon. In the Apple case the network revolves around association with the Apple brand (*i.e.* around the perception that different kinds of people use Macs than use PCs). Such associations may also become valuable in the online video marketplace, placing a trusted intermediary between the studios and the consumers. The success of iTunes in transferring a sizable segment of the illegal music download market into the legal market may illustrate this potential in creating viable online markets.

But it is the interactive elements of the social network phenomenon that could be its most important value-generating potential. For example, commercial film producers could use feedback from social networks to plan the content and timing of film and video productions with more precision (*Financial Times* 2006c, Ritson 2006, Klaessen 2005, *Business Week* 2005). Also, in principle, social network sites could provide smaller independent producers with a venue for releasing their product (in whole or in part) and for receiving the kinds of feedback from audiences that might otherwise be available only from expensive market research.

The rapidly increasing corporate interest in social networks may affect the dynamics and use of the major sites. MySpace is now owned by News Corporation and in October 2006 Google paid USD 1.65 billion for YouTube. But these two corporations have very different basic business models; News Corporation is primarily a content company, whereas Google is primarily a 'navigation' company connecting users with providers. The YouTube acquisition illustrates how new entrants to the content market are likely to encounter turbulence. Immediately upon acquiring YouTube, copyright infringement claims were filed against Google regarding content that had been uploaded to YouTube (*Financial Times* 2006d). As other types of businesses enter this market – for example, telecommunication operators or software companies – further turbulence would appear likely. It appears certain that different corporate strategies will compete to acquire stakes in this emerging Internet phenomenon and to shape its commercial potential. Use of social networks by major studios and television networks indicates that they are now regarded as valuable new points of market entry for commercial film and video content. But also, these networks are potentially important sources of commercially valuable information *about* consumers of audio-visual products.

Emerging new roles for digital rights management (DRM)

Digital rights management is certain to play a major role in the development virtually all distribution modalities for digital film and video content. However, although essential to combat counterfeiting and piracy, the full future significance of DRM is likely to be strategic as well as protective.

The environment for digital distribution described above is highly fluid. Particularly in the downloading segment, business and pricing models appear to change frequently, indicating that many of them are exploratory or experimental. The key new issue for the industry in general is to discover what the consumer will buy, in what format, at what price and, crucially, in which consumption *context,* of which now there is a large and expanding variety.

In order to exploit the full commercial potential of digital content, publishers must be able not only to protect it from thieves, but also to position it in different consumption contexts at different levels of consumer value. For example, it is reasonable to assume that access to a newly released feature film in an up-sampled version suitable for high-resolution display on state-of-the-art home entertainment systems would represent more value to the consumer than a down-sampled version intended for distribution to mobile telephones. Likewise, a single play rental would represent a different level of value than an unlimited play agreement. Were prices to vary accordingly, this could give positive signals to a variety of emerging markets.

At this time, however, positioning content in this way exposes the content provider to risk that content provided in one context will be expropriated illegally and transferred to other contexts. Accordingly, DRM technology is required that will specify not just the terms of use (*e.g.* the rental period) but also the particular device or devices on which it will be played. As DRM technologies become more sophisticated, more product offerings with 'menu' pricing schemes adjusted to various consumption environments can be expected.

The online video future

Overall, the full potential of online video distribution may not be realised in the short to medium term. Furthemore, the corporate and investment structure of the media industries generally is heavily oriented to enhanced cable television systems as well as to online environments which means that they have high sunk costs in current high-volume systems. Also, concerns about piracy and counterfeiting have meant that many of the online distribution models must use DRM regimes that may require consumers to use digital content in ways that appear more restrictive than DVD purchases or rentals. The most significant observation about the current state of online distribution is that there are many publishers of many descriptions that are experimenting with many models. As a result, no entirely coherent approach to this market has yet emerged and several problems of technological co-ordination persist. However, the online environment may be used also in order to develop entirely new interactive relationships between content consumers and publishers that may become as or more commercially significant than downloading as such. In particular, the potential of social networks bears watching in this regard.

The costs of digital film and video production

Conversion to a fully digital production and distribution environment is well underway and cost reduction is cited often as one of the major stimuli. But actually there are few data about digital production costs. However, a recent Canadian survey (Sears *et al.* 2006) offers several insights. As a high proportion of both television and film production in Canada is for major US studios, these trends may be indicative for the industry as a whole. The study estimated that for lower-budget, mainly television-oriented Canadian-produced content, 73% of productions over approximately a 10-year period used tape and only 19% used film. Only 3% of video productions were in digital format and only one-third of these in high definition. Likewise, tape was the most preferred post-production and distribution medium (84% of projects). In complete contrast, large-budget features overwhelmingly preferred film as the production medium (85% of projects). In the post-production and distribution segments, however, distribution was split. In the post-production segment 49% preferred tape and 45% preferred film. In the distribution segment 50% preferred tape and 45% preferred film. In the post-production segment, however, digital technology virtually replaced analogue in this period.

These data show that despite technological advances, the choice of production medium is mostly determined by whether content is for cinema or TV and by the associated distribution and exhibition structures. Producers also associate different types of content with different qualities of cinematographic image, and are much more likely to choose high-definition video for dramatic features and nature programs than for short programs or television series. The Sears report indicated that the average cost differential for dramatic, documentary and children's television programming is approximately 25% more for high definition than for standard definition. and that variety and performing arts programming is more than twice as expensive to produce in high definition. As cinema production and high definition television are virtually equivalent, it can be assumed that digital production of cinema films may also generate additional costs (Figure 5.5).

Figure 5.5. Average cost differentials between standard definition and high definition television production in Canada 2004-2005 (CAD millions)

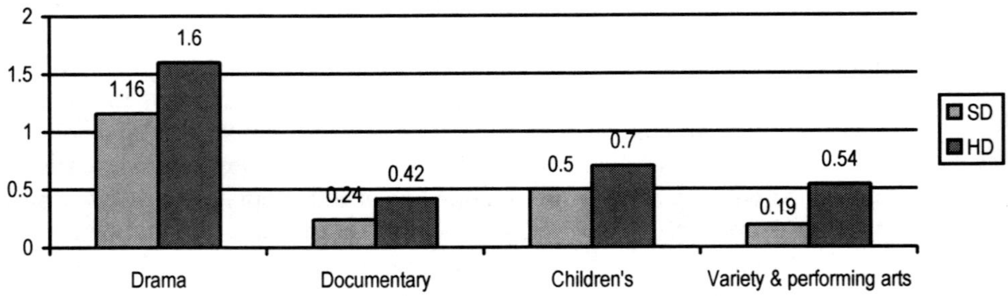

Source: CFTPA (2006). Data apply only to productions supported by the Canadian Television Fund.

Especially for cinema content, the main immediate advantage claimed for digital production is savings on duplication and distribution. However, the Sears report noted that producers identify several sources of savings and costs, most of them related to the type of production, its budget and intended market. Most savings were reported to come from production and post-production efficiencies, especially from the closer integration of the shooting schedule with special effects and editing functions that follows from the elimination of analogue-digital-analogue conversion in the editing segment. But others noted that the cost (rental or purchase) of digital production equipment is higher and that HD tape stock is much more costly than SD stock, although this cost is likely to disappear with more widespread use of direct to disc image capture. There was also concern that digital production breeds its own inefficiencies, such as time-consuming data processing.

The other possible source of escalating costs is human resources. Regardless of whether the production environment is digital or analogue, many of the same functions in the film-making process remain. For example, live action films will retain all of the mechanical trades irrespective of how the images are captured. Likewise, even though the post-production segments are virtually fully digitised, a production still requires a film editor, sound editor, composer, etc. In other words, although the production environment may be recapitalised, most of this investment remains tied directly to human skills. Moreover, as the film and video industries are characterised by low labour substitutability (see Chapter 2) premiums for high-reputation workers are unlikely to disappear.

Indeed, human resource costs may increase substantially in the digital environment. Although there are no data on wage differentials between digital and analogue production, there is no necessary reason to assume a reduction in the number of required workers or in their wages. First, in a situation of a low labour substitutability, established workers who acquire new skills may well demand higher fees (especially if they are unionised). Second, as indicated in Table 5.5, many of the digital production skills in high demand may themselves add new types of technological value to the production process. For example, post-production contractors who develop new or improved software may be in positions to demand fees for IP licenses and to drive these fees up.

Table 5.5. Film and video skills in decline and in demand

Skills in decline	Skills in demand
Flatbed editing	Digital production
Linear/analogue editing	Computer-generated imagery (CGI)
Post-production on film	3D graphics and special effects
Analogue sound mixing	Digital animation
Negative cutting	Video editing
Film camera operation	Computer-aided design (CAD)

Source: Sears *et al.* (2006).

The final cost issue concerns *digital permanence*. Barring destruction, all motion pictures on film stock have high permanence and can be read with more or less the same technology. Moreover, they can be scanned and rescanned into other formats and still retain their essential data. The same cannot be said for digital images and sound. Even if there are no mechanical problems (*e.g.* degradation or contamination of storage media), file and transport standards and DRM codes change frequently. In all electronic media it is becoming recognised that digital content is highly ephemeral by nature, requiring extensive and costly regimes to preserve formats or update files into new formats as they appear on the market. Film products historically have had long shelf lives, and the increasing opportunities for content owners to exploit archives as well as new productions highlight the permanence issue.

Chapter 6

DIGITAL FILM AND VIDEO CONTENT AND FUTURE VALUE CHAIN EVOLUTION

Despite very significant technological evolution beginning with the very first narrative motion picture, the value-added structure of the production segments of the film and video industry has undergone only minor adjustment. Many reasons for this stability relate to the high human resource intensity of film and video products. There has been considerably greater structural evolution in the non-production segments of the value chain – especially in the exhibition and auxiliary streams. In fairly rapid succession, technologies such as video cassettes, DVDs and online downloads supported entirely new rental and sell-through business models. Similar opportunities have come with new generations of television (particularly pay-TV) and video-on-demand. These new sources of value-added are now essential to the return-on-investment structure.

This chapter explores how the value chain may evolve even further over the next 5-10 years, and what the implications of these changes could be. The extent and speed of change in the value chain is likely to increase as the remaining analogue bottlenecks in the production and post-production segments are eliminated, and as the emergence of industry-wide standards encourages the wider adoption of new technology throughout the value chain.

The effects of full digitisation on the value chain

As the remaining analogue bottlenecks disappear, major effects on the value chain seem likely to occur in five main areas. Three of these involve mostly truncation, amalgamation, reorganisation or redefinition of existing value-added segments and/or enhanced interactions between segments. But two entirely new value added streams seem poised to emerge also, one a product of emerging data archiving requirements and the other a product of interactive social networking capabilities.

Truncation and reorganisation of the production and post-production segments

Full digitisation of all production and post-production segments will allow much closer integration of these segments, virtually in real time. Key to this is the elimination of analogue image capture and provision of direct digital feeds between production and post-production segments without analogue-digital conversion. In principle, this makes it possible to assemble each section of a film in much more complete form at each production stage. This enhanced facility may create production efficiencies by eliminating the costs and time lags associated with the processing of film and through more efficient co-ordination and sequencing of special effects and animation. These developments may also lower production costs for smaller independent producers such that they do not present as great a barrier to market entry and they facilitate a lighter-weight production process for some types of products.

Digitisation also may create opportunities to *market* filmed entertainment products in new ways. The most obvious opportunity is to release (perhaps online via social networks) short 'enticements' while production is still underway. A strategy of 'gradual release' could also be used to gather early audience feedback, helping to indicate optimal release strategies (Ritson 2006). Fully digital production also suggests possible new direct and dynamic links with auxiliary value chain segments, particularly games and spin-offs in other media.

Redefinition and possible relocation of the duplication segment

Most analogue film duplication is performed by a small handful of specialist companies, and most feature films are printed by only two companies, Technicolor and Deluxe. Owing to the cost implications of making and delivering projection prints, this function traditionally has been situated with the advertising, promotion and distribution functions (the print & advertising stream) mostly controlled by the distributing studio (major or independent). If digital cinema technology reduces the marginal costs of the 'print' function to virtually nothing, then the duplication function may evolve into little more than issuing a license to exhibit. Already duplication companies are converting their businesses: providing digital imaging quality control or technical services as part of the shooting and processing segments.

In this new environment, once a film is completed the producer can simply feed the file directly to the distributing studio, or distribute it directly to cinemas, television program packagers, DVD manufacturers and so forth. However, neither the producer nor the distributor may want to manage what would become essentially a very large data-archiving enterprise. This may create a market for outsourcing the storage and management of digital motion picture content, thus creating an entirely new value chain segment. These decisions may be determined also by 'permanence' considerations where third-party companies may offer special management and technical skills to keep digital content archives upgraded to new data formats and file transfer standards.

Redefinition and re-assignment of the distribution segment

Digital distribution could provide much the same technical distribution efficiencies for cinema as have always applied to television, with digital cinema files delivered to distributors on public communication networks in the same way as programs are distributed to television broadcasters. As most technical distribution functions in a digital production environment concern network configuration and management, the technical distribution function eventually could be devolved mostly to telecommunication carriers.

Closer integration of the cinema and television exhibition segments

The primary historical distinctions between film and video products concern the exhibition media and the business models. By eliminating technical differences in the ways cinema and television products are made and distributed, there could be much greater integration of the two markets. For example, there could be much more dynamic selection and distribution by different types of exhibitors. Some operators of digital cinema screens are already experimenting with programming that has not commonly been consumed in cinemas. There may also be much more dynamic selection of media, with both cinema exhibitors and television broadcasters bidding competitively for certain types of content, or showing some of the same content. Alternatively, a film that delivers a disappointing first cinema weekend may be transferred more quickly to television, or a made-for-TV film that draws a huge audience on pay-TV may quickly be transferred to cinema screens.

Creation of a new 'communications' value-added segment

There is a particularly intriguing role for the Internet in developing new value chain segments. Most immediately, interactive communication modalities and social networks provide an entirely new set of tools for real-time, value-added communication between producers and consumers of film and video products, and for the development of new and highly sophisticated feedback mechanisms. This capability looks certain to emerge despite the current competitive and technical barriers to the rapid development of online video distribution as outlined in Chapter 5, and likely it will be stimulated by the increasing take-up of dedicated devices such as the iPod, and of mobile devices more generally, particularly mobile TV.

There are very real commercial advantages in exploiting the same product in different media, multiplying the value of each media product rather than reducing value through 'convergence' upon single multi-purpose platforms. The film and video industries have exploited such neighbouring market strategies extremely successfully such that these markets now produce much of the return on investment from a cinema product and substantial additional returns from television programming. What has been missing to this point is an effective, real-time and self-organising mechanism to gather and link commercial intelligence from all of these various markets. In principle, this makes social networks valuable to advertisers in trying to target specific consumers as network participants not only upload and download content, but in the process also provide information about themselves and their preferences to producers. For these reasons, the online environment is potentially the source of a new value-added stream that spans both the processes involved in making a filmed entertainment product and in exhibiting and exploiting it in various commercial contexts.

Value chain evolution and industry structure

Chapter 3 showed that despite relative stability in the value chain as such, the structure of the film and video *industries* has evolved considerably over the past 10-15 years. Many brand names have remained but the ownership, corporate, project, financial and exhibition structures have all undergone major changes. Most productions now typically involve the intensive co-ordination of inputs from many independent companies. The digital production environment promises to make this form of organisation more efficient, but the changing technological nature of the motion picture product may also make relationships between these stakeholders even more complex.

It was noted in Chapter 3 that the increasing incidence of domestic and international co-production potentially results in more rapid knowledge transfer to potential competitors. This can create incentives for companies currently in the market to innovate in order to remain competitive, but it also may stimulate new entrants, especially if the basic entry costs are lessened by the availability of low-cost, high-quality digital production technologies and the wider availability of independent specialist collaborators. New entrant opportunities may be stimulated further by exhibitor experimentation with new forms of film and video products in order to exploit more of the potential of digital cinema.

New *technology* markets may also open up within the production structure. Computer-based production processes can be improved incrementally with software, some of which may be developed directly by the professionals and technicians who provide production and post-production services. As many functions are now performed by contractors or production partners, there will be a much more complex contractual structure that can include IPR options and licensing agreements for production services in addition to normal service performance obligations.

The role of the major studios is also likely to change in a fully digitised value chain. But considering the extensive real or potential links that now exist between film and video producers and other media outlets and networks, the studios may even rise in importance. The venture capital-like structure of film financing means that the digital environment may offer studios enhanced dynamic capabilities to reallocate products to different media markets, such that the overall performance of each film portfolio can be enhanced. Furthermore, the potential of social video networks may challenge conventional markets by further fragmenting the range of film and video services available to consumers.

On the other hand, the traditional role of large studios in market-making and branding may be weakened with lower-cost independent production, redefinition or virtual elimination of the duplication cycle, and significant changes in distribution both to cinema audiences and online users. Full digitisation of the film and video *supply* chain appears already to have stimulated digital cinema operators to explore new forms of content and to develop new value-added streams for their exhibition facilities – sports, educational and business-related content, for example. This may result eventually in a cinema exhibition sector that defines itself more broadly than only a conduit for studio productions.

Value chain evolution and commercial strategies

Much of the discussion concerning the digitisation of film and video content stresses efficiency and cost issues. Information technology is often presented as a vehicle for production and distribution efficiencies in order for existing producers to remain competitive and for new ones to become competitive. However, although there is potential for efficiency gains, the analysis in this study suggests strongly that the greatest value in digitising film and video content lies in creating new commercial relationships between film and video products, their consumers and their producers. Certainly this is confirmed by the actions of the major media conglomerates in acquiring or redistributing stakes in new media, particularly in the various networking sectors. Up to this point, the strategy has mostly involved creating new ways to multiply revenues from existing and new products. But signs are emerging that the value in various segments will soon be exploited in new ways, many involving interactive communication with consumers and users, and within the production and distribution structures themselves. Furthermore, content digitisation increases opportunities for value-added intermediation in production and distribution based on new skills.

Value chain evolution and the economic viability of filmed entertainment

In Chapter 2 it was shown that many of the unique economic features of the film and video industries stem from the 'experience goods' characteristics of these products, whose market performance depends on complex interactions between psychological, social and cultural factors. The basic trade-off that was noted between production quality and the propensity of a filmed entertainment product to attract an audience would seem to be maintained in a digital environment. Although the sources and types of costs may be shifting, the overall ratio of investment to return would appear not to be changing. Even though most of the high-cost elements that are not associated with performers are fully digital already (e.g. computer-generated imagery and special effects), the theatrical cost of feature films continues to escalate.

Interactive relationships with consumers and users may change some of this. Currently for feature films, the strategy is to establish the property through cinema exhibition and then to exploit neighbouring markets (alternative distribution media) and after-markets (associated merchandise). However, new sequencing models may develop for some product types as film and video enterprises learn to assess and exploit the social dynamics of new forms of consumer interaction.

Ultimately, there remains the question of whether or not the digital production environment will increase the quantity of new film and video content overall. The function of major film studios and broadcasting networks is to produce and distribute content, but historically these decisions have respected various 'quality' thresholds in accordance with consumer preferences. There are strong economic arguments that simply increasing the number of productions could lower these thresholds on some types of products, thus actually reducing the likelihood that each additional product will achieve a sufficient return on investment. For these reasons, it seems likely that overall production levels for feature films and television programming will continue to follow already established output patterns, with production increases likely to come in the form of entirely new types of content, aided by lower cost and higher quality digital content creation and distribution technologies.

Chapter 7

THE POLICY FRAMEWORK

Until comparatively recently, the film and video industry in most OECD countries has been treated mainly within a 'cultural industry' framework. Once embodied in a digital data file, however, film and video content becomes associated with a much broader range of economic and industry policies. Increasingly, more governments are coming to regard the film and video industries as highly productive economic activities within a growing constellation of Internet-enabled technologies and services.

This chapter examines some of the most common policy areas and approaches in the light of the analysis presented in the previous chapters, focussing on some current national or regional policy initiatives.

Innovation and technology

Research and development

The digitisation of film and video content increases the technology intensity of the industry, particularly regarding advanced high value-added services, especially software. This makes the industry more R&D-intensive. All OECD countries offer various forms of R&D support, ranging from tax incentives to subsidies, and such schemes are applied to a wide range of technologies, many of which are relevant to further development of the digital audio-visual environment. Very substantial R&D-intensive technology and services markets can be expected to develop in order to support the merging of cinema and video production environments, the development of digital cinema, and online distribution methods. Already several countries that are not significant exporters of film and video products as such have acquired comparative advantages in key related technology markets (*e.g.* Japan and Korea in studio production technologies, digital projection and advanced consumer electronics).

Entirely new film and video distribution and exhibition formats tend to emerge relatively infrequently and the history of R&D strategies in the audiovisual sector has been that countries whose industries capture these markets first are those that stay at the technological forefront over many cycles of experimentation and are prepared to sustain their investment over periods of low apparent consumer interest. For example, high-definition television first emerged in the mid-1980s but is only now generating a significant market, spurred by developments in broadband networking, digital video imaging and storage formats, digital broadcasting and home cinema systems. The few mostly Asian and European firms (*e.g.* Sony and Thomson) with long-term commitments to these technologies are now set to reap the rewards.

Human resource development

All OECD countries have human resource development strategies and advanced training programs, many undertaken in conjunction with specialised business associations and the private sector, and there are notable examples of initiatives relevant specifically to the film and video industries. As these industries are human resource-intensive, a highly skilled local workforce is essential in order for a country or region not just to attract motion picture productions (which can require nothing more than positional assets like scenery), but to maximise and retain value from them. This is possible only if there are highly skilled local contractors and crews, especially in high value-added production and post-production segments, who can acquire a reputation in the industry internationally for the quality and creativity of their work. This strategy has been pursued to good effect in the UK, New Zealand, Germany, Australia, Canada, Japan and Korea, particularly regarding animation software and computer-generated images (CGI).

Developing and keeping these skills may require public investment and several countries now offer substantial support. For example, in Canada there are now 33 film and video trade training facilities spread among six provinces. In Australia, AUD 9 million has been earmarked over three years for the Australian Film, Television and Radio School, one of the principal objectives being to deliver multiplatform courses and to establish a national Screen Business Skills Centre to complement existing internship support schemes and industry apprenticeships. This follows on previous long-term commitments from the 1970s onwards to develop the industry.

However, given the increasing R&D intensity of the film and video industry, one of the main planning questions for human resource policy concerns whether the highest value skills are those applied directly to film and video production, or those related more to basic and applied research into advanced information technologies that may find applications in the film and video industries. National policies that are oriented only to film and video applications and not to linking the production base in this industry with the broader science and technology base may be less effective in the longer run.

Business and regulatory environment

Competition

Most OECD countries have media ownership and competition policies, largely based upon the rationale that governments have a public responsibility to ensure diversity of content and opinion. Historically these policies have been expressed in terms of restrictions on ownership, both regarding foreign ownership and regarding shares of specific local markets and cross-ownership of different media. These types of controls can be exerted through regulation and licensing (*e.g.* broadcast licenses). In some markets however, for example in Australia, and in the US following the loosening of media ownership restrictions during the last Clinton administration, the possibility of greater concentration of ownership within and between media has increased.

In the film and video segment particularly, regulation has applied to breaking up vertical integration and exclusivity between cinema production and distribution, and restricting local concentration of ownership mostly concerning broadcast television. However, many anomalies remain. For example, cable television franchises are still local monopolies in most OECD countries. Competition policy in the cinema segment is less straightforward. Unlike terrestrial and cable broadcasters, cinema operators do not require special licenses. The location of cinema facilities is subject more to local planning regulations than to national or international policy regimes.

With increasing content digitisation and digital delivery, new challenges to competition policies are emerging. Many historical issues of cross-ownership and segment integration are now more difficult to isolate in that most film and video products are increasingly fungible between the distribution undertakings of many different companies. Digital cinema conversion provides another example of new challenges. Specifically this concerns the issue of conversion costs in the exhibition segment that are subsidised by equipment manufacturers and/or production studios. Such tied arrangements could re-establish vertical integration of a different kind, favouring some kinds of product over others and reducing the separation between equipment and content.

In addition, digital content is becoming valuable in different ways to a much wider spectrum of commercial interests, as exemplified by the increasing carriage of copyrighted audio-visual material by third-party distributors. The economic viability of Apple's iPod approach to video downloads depends on access to copyright film and video content on a basis that fits their business model (or the models of competitor systems being introduced by Sony, Microsoft and others). Copyright holders are fully entitled to discriminate in terms of which companies distribute their products electronically. Currently a wide range of new licensing arrangements to distribute video content are being explored, many of which may have the potential to change competitive conditions and access in video markets (see OECD, 2006d). Similar issues are developing with the rapid uptake of social networks, where a wide range of content copyright, ownership and use issues with potentially important competition implications are being raised (see OECD 2007c).

Trade

The import-export environment for film and video products has been reshaped in recent years by international trade agreements and trade-in-services treaties at regional and global levels (*e.g.* NAFTA and the WTO). Historically, national policies for the film and video industries in many OECD countries have been predicated upon assumptions that producers in local markets were disadvantaged by the global dynamics of the industry, and particularly by the very large production capacity of the English-language cluster. This has led to continuing and ongoing debates about whether local markets require protection, or in which circumstances cultural factors should override economic and trade principles.

However, more countries are now acquiring a significant share in the production and co-production of internationally successful entertainment products and more products are now being exported from more countries. Furthermore, in some cases the internationalisation of production between OECD countries can be linked with substantially increased production capacity aimed at domestic markets (Canada and the UK are good examples). Nevertheless, quotas and restrictions on film and video products still apply in many countries, notably outside the OECD. For example, in 2006 the MPAA identified a number of continuing trade barriers and market access barriers including limits on foreign ownership, taxation, advertising, dubbing requirements and high import duties, in addition to IPR legislation, enforcement and protection issues (MPAA, 2006).

Overall, recent developments would suggest that in a digital content environment, trade should be seen not just in terms of the import and export of audio-visual products as such, but also in terms of acquiring shares in the international organisation and division of labour in this industry, especially in high value-added segments.

Cultural issues

There has been a long history intertwining cultural and trade factors in media policy. OECD countries have pursued media policies variously on the assumption either that an increase in national cultural strength will yield greater production and export of media products, or that an increase in the production of media products will yield increased cultural visibility.

In many cases, policy must also take account of cultural and linguistic sensitivities. The issue is particularly important in the European Union, where the task of building a single internal market encounters a wide range of linguistic and ethnic media constituencies spread across 25 countries. EU policy promotes cultural diversity, *e.g.* by promoting a more aggregated European film and video marketplace. At the European level, the Media 2007 program encourages digitalisation of audio-visual content and the e-Content initiative promotes access to digital content in multilingual environments.

The online environment may increase the scope for both production and distribution of content relevant to smaller and/or more local cultural markets. This may also occur within countries that are already major exporters of media content. Independent and experimental producers in large countries face many of the same challenges as do similar producers in smaller countries. In the new environment, policy may need to shift from cultural policies based upon static protective measures towards more pro-active measures to encourage and promote experimentation and cultural diversity, especially where it is possible to tie new forms of content creation with new exhibition and distribution technologies.

Infrastructure

Broadband and content

All OECD countries place a high priority on widespread rollout and use of high-speed Internet facilities. The continuing growth of high-speed broadband coverage and use is an essential factor in the ongoing creation, distribution and use of digital film and video content. High-speed links are required for the digital production process and for new digital cinema technologies, as well as for e-commerce, online content distribution and the development of social video network sites. This implies that substantial and continuing technical harmonisation and upgrading in the underlying broadband network environment is necessary if many of the commercial models for online film and video distribution are to develop and grow.

There is a continuing debate on how the new high-speed broadband infrastructure should be financed and how and at what levels services should be priced. For example, providers of high-bandwidth services (like video downloading sites) or high-volume facilities (like browsers) eventually could pay different prices for higher bandwidth access arrangements that would enable providers to deliver more real-time, bandwidth-intensive video over the Internet at a potentially greater scale and scope. This debate over what is often called 'network neutrality' is ongoing and heated, although few agree precisely what network neutrality really means. Nevertheless, the debate and any potential outcomes, in all their iterations, could have major implications for the delivery of digital multimedia content and the provision of innovative high-bandwidth services. The traditional economic model of the film and video industries depends on careful self-regulation of quality, cost, quantity and timing factors. However, the evolution of broadband has led to the growth of diverse new media generation models, including user-generated content. This may not have major effects on production rates, particularly for new feature film and video content in the short term, but it could have profound effects on experimentation, potential new entrants, and evolving methods of content distribution and access.

Obtaining greater distribution for archived film and video products and exploiting the interactive dynamics of social networks are two important emerging market opportunities for increasing and diversifying legal download markets. Both of these may require policy attention, the first because in many countries a great deal of important archived film and video material has been generated or is stocked in the public sector (see OECD 2006c) and second because it raises a range of policy issues, like privacy and security, that lie over and above broadband access and use (see OECD 2007c).

Conversion costs

Conversion to a digital film and video production environment requires complementary investments in distribution and consumption devices and in many cases both commercial users and private consumers of these products must make new capital investments in new technologies. For example, high-definition digital television is available only via appropriately equipped terminals in which the user must make the investment. Various OECD governments have in the past acted to regulate this conversion in order to fairly distribute these costs over a reasonable time period. In the UK, for example, definite time lines were established for the conversion from analogue to digital radio and television broadcasting in the 'free-to-air' segment.

Business development

Industry promotion

Most OECD governments are active in promoting their national film and video industries, both in terms of producing and exporting domestic products, and attracting contract and co-productions from foreign countries. Many schemes are oriented directly to public sector support for the commercial film industry, but several of these are re-orienting specifically to the digital environment.

Japan is promoting digital content through the creation in 2004 of the Visual Industry Promotion Organisation (VIPO), which was modelled on 'film boards' as found in other countries (*e.g.* the British Film Council, the Korean Film Council and the American Film Institute). VIPO provides support for the development of human resources in co-operation with educational institutions, subsidises studio costs and encourages entrepreneurship in developing domestic and global markets for Japanese film and video products. In a similar vein, the Spanish Institute of Cinematography and Audiovisual Arts (ICAA) has an incentive scheme to support independent distributors to make Spanish-language films available for digital distribution. Funding is by agreement with the Instituto de Crédito Oficial (a public finance institution) whereby 'soft' loans (*i.e.* with partially subsidised interest) subsidise conventional and online distribution.

Australia likewise has launched an industry-led, government-supported Digital Content Industry Action Agenda which focuses on attracting investment for digital production, export promotion, skills development and R&D. The initiative includes an investment scoping forum to bring producers and investors together, an industry capability map to evaluate industry strengths and an investment guide for SMEs in the digital industries. A range of Australian and state government agencies and programs also promote conversion to digital content by providing grants to film, animation, special effects and the games industry. New Zealand has a similar digital strategy that encompasses the creation of a digital policy framework, and a program to build up a standardised technical architecture for access to domestic digital content resources. In Canada, federal funding is available specifically for the development of digital content and the New Media Research Networks Fund supports innovative applied research linking technology with the cultural industries. Specific to digital content in the Canadian, Australian and New Zealand initiatives is the substantial focus on acquiring market share in development of underlying technologies and not just the subsidy of domestic film and video productions.

Production subsidies and incentives

Several OECD countries currently offer tax concessions and other subsidies specifically for film and video production. These subsidise some of the production expenses of domestic producers and/or are used to attract foreign investment in the form of contract or location shooting. Typically these incentives are designed such that they enhance returns to investors, domestic and foreign, while at the same time providing a more stable economic underpinning for locally based film producers and contractors. Box 7.1 outlines the recently overhauled fiscal incentive framework in Australia, which illustrates many basic structural features that will also be found in other OECD jurisdictions. However, the Australian approach is innovative in that it ties fiscal incentive programs to closer integration of the overall funding and support structure for the industry.

Inward subsidies and incentives have often been discussed in connection with possible trade distortions and competition between locations that offer the highest subsidies. However, financial inducements *alone* without the development of the complementary human resources and related infrastructures are probably not sufficient to yield local benefits except in the very short term. For productions that are outsourced to more peripheral locations, arguably the greatest level of economic spin-off is obtained when studio and post-production facilities can be found in these locales also.

Moreover, many of these incentives are not offered by national governments. In North America, for example, both US states and Canadian provinces have considerable independent tax-raising powers, and film and video producers can obtain tax incentives and other subsidies at local and regional levels. These fiscal incentives can generate intense competition between regions within as well as between countries. Often individual cities in the same country compete with each other to become attractive as production locations. Locally based schemes are popular and are considered in many cases to have realised returns to local economies that are well in excess of those from similar concessions granted to other types of industries. These new developments reflect the increasingly global production system.

Box 7.1. Recent industry promotion measures: The Australian Screen Production Incentive

In May 2007, as part of the 2007-2008 budget, the Australian government announced a comprehensive package of measures designed to strengthen the film and television industry. The package has three major components.

A new producer rebate scheme has been introduced, aimed at Australian productions. The producer rebate will provide a financial incentive to producers of Australian film and television projects, giving them the capacity to offer significant returns to investors for productions with demonstrated market appeal. Projects will be eligible to access the rebate where they are 'creatively' controlled by Australians and meet minimum qualifying expenditure thresholds. Eligible feature films will receive a rebate of 40% of their qualifying Australian production expenditure. Eligible productions for other media, principally television drama, will receive a 20% rebate. These productions will include television movies, mini-series and new long-form television series.

A new location rebate scheme, which is an enhanced refundable film tax offset, is aimed at attracting overseas productions to Australia. The location rebate will replace the refundable film tax offset scheme with an increased rebate of 15%. It will also be extended to include expenditure on post-production, digital and visual effects that are undertaken in Australia and valued at over AUD 5 million. Both the producer rebate scheme and the location rebate scheme are uncapped and will be administered through the taxation system.

The third component is the creation from 1 July 2008 of a new screen agency incorporating the Australian Film Commission, the Film Finance Corporation and Film Australia Limited. A government review found that the existing film agencies were operating efficiently and effectively with each agency recording some very significant achievements in recent years. However, the introduction of a strong alternative funding mechanism through the producer rebate provides scope to bring together the functions of the three agencies. This will ensure that one body is positioned to consider strategic industry priorities and take a holistic approach to funding Australian productions.

Intellectual property rights

In many places in this study, attention has been drawn to IPR issues. The basic problem is how to facilitate access and use of digital content and to exploit new business models, while preventing illegal use. Much of this debate has focussed upon digital rights management, but as discussed in Chapter 5, DRM provides only limited protection and, moreover, plays an increasingly important strategic role in providing consumers with choices as to how they acquire and digital content.

Current IPR concerns about counterfeiting and piracy are shaped by the very low marginal reproduction cost characteristics of digital content. In the digital environment, the issue is not simply misuse or theft as such, but that such activity can be turned into profit more efficiently because of low marginal reproduction costs and imperfect traceability methods. However, although each media has its own special IPR concerns, in a digital environment these problems are generic rather than media-specific. Rather than piecemeal solutions for each individual – and rapidly changing – medium, solutions are needed that will foil counterfeiting and piracy in digital media as a whole. OECD governments recognise the need for a workable regime to combat counterfeiting and piracy that will not permit unauthorised commercialising of copyrighted content or excessive copying, but which will also take account of principles of fair use (see OECD 2005b, 2005c, 2006b, 2007a and 2007c).

Some emerging IPR issues that are specific to the film and video industry are related to the development of new standards. Initiatives such as DCI are striving to bring industry-wide standards to the digital production environment. However, the range of potential technology stakeholders is much broader than the audio-visual industry. For example, the Advanced Access Content System is a content distribution standard to control access to and copying of the next generation of optical discs and DVDs, involving the consumer electronics and software industries as well as film and video industries. This diversity of interests suggests that there will be ongoing competition on technology and standards, and IPR legal challenges in film and video distribution along the lines of those surrounding wireless Internet services. The evolving distributed production structure of the industry is also likely to lead to greater original IPR inputs (in software) from a wider range of industry participants, thus raising further IPR issues. IPR concerns also figure prominently in the digital permanence debate, which must deal with problems created by proprietary formats.

DRM systems are designed to tackle some of these issues by providing consumer access to content while protecting intellectual property (OECD 2005e). The simultaneous availability of incompatible systems with different video file formats and encoding and compression techniques, plus the fact that not all systems can access content from all providers, may create confusion for consumers and vendors and add to total consumer and producer costs. Overall, this area requires continuing development and rationalisation if, for example, digital downloading services are to reach their potential.

Part of the solution to these problems may lie with initiatives like the *European Charter for the Development and Take-up of Film Online*, a European regional initiative involving representatives of the audio-visual content industry, Internet service providers and telecom operators. Adopted on 23 May 2006, the Charter promotes examples of commendable practices in several areas, such as commercial agreements between content providers and online service providers (including revenues, release windows and rights clearance), joint actions aiming at increasing consumer education and copyright awareness, and co-operation to fight piracy (including development of technologies to protect copyrighted material).

Conceptualisation, classification and measurement

Further work is needed on a range of conceptual and classification issues. Despite the blurring of some boundaries – particularly in terms of distribution platforms where many different kinds of content can be delivered over the same platforms – current classification systems do not distinguish clearly between film and video products and other kinds of audio-visual products such as commercials, music videos or industrial promotion and training materials which belong to other value chains (*e.g.* advertising, music, human resource development) and only incidentally use some of the same technologies for their production. Better definition of these different activities and identification of their origin and final use would add greatly to analysis of the full impacts of digital film and video products.

Policy challenges

Spurred in large measure by governments promoting information technologies and the Internet as engines of economic growth, the line between film and video policy and general 'information economy' or 'information society' policies has become blurred. The new challenge for governments is to devise approaches to balancing these evolving agendas in the public interest. In many cases this may not require the implementation of entirely new types of policies or policy-driven industry initiatives, but rather the shaping and redirection of existing policy to reflect the emerging new realities of these industries. In other cases, established policy approaches and attitudes may become less relevant, particularly taking into account the global nature of creation, production, distribution and use of film and video products.

Bibliography

Afuah, A. and C. Tucci (2001), *Internet Business Models and Strategies*, Boston, McGraw Hill.

Albert S. (1999), "Movie Stars and the Distribution of Financially Successful Films in the Motion Picture Industry – A Reply", *Journal of Cultural Economics*, 23, pp. 325-329.

Altman, E., S. Goyal and S. Sahu (2006), "A Digital Media Asset Ecosystem for the Global Film Industry", *Journal of Digital Asset Management*, 2, pp. 6-16.

Bell, A. (1999), "The Dynamic Digital Disk", *IEEE Spectrum*, October, pp. 28-35.

Business Week (2005), "Murdoch's Web Gambit", 10 October, p. 34.

Cassidy, R. (1933), "Some Economic Aspects of Motion Picture Production and Marketing, *The Journal of Business of the University of Chicago*, 6 (2), pp. 113-131.

Caves R. E. (2000), *Creative Industries – Contract between Art and Commerce*, Harvard University Press, Cambridge, Massachusetts.

CFTPA (2006), *Profile 2006 - An Economic Report on the Canadian Film and Television Production Industry*, Canadian Film and Television Producers Association.

Cherry, S. M. (2002), "Lost and Found: Media Sales", *IEEE Spectrum*, July, p. 45.

Chesbrough, H. and R. S. Rosenbloom (2002) ,"The Role of the Business Model in Capturing Value from Innovation: Evidence from Xerox Corporation's Technology Spin-off Companies", *Industrial and Corporate Change,* June, 11 (3) 529-555.

Commission of the European Communities (2001), Commission staff working paper on certain legal aspects relating to cinematographic and other audiovisual works, Brussels, 11 April.

Currah, A. (2003), "Digital Effects in the Spatial Economy of Film: Towards a Research Agenda, *Area*, 35 (1), pp. 64-73.

Cook, D. and W. Wang (2004), "Neutralizing the Piracy of Motion Pictures: Re-engineering the Industry's Supply Chain", *Technology in Society,* 26, pp. 567–583.

DCI (2005), Digital Cinema System Specification Version 1.0, July 10, Digital Cinema Initiatives, LLC Member Representatives Committee.

Dettmer, R. (2003), "Digital Cinema: A Slow Revolution", *IEE Review*, November, pp. 46-50.

Debande, O. and G. Chetrit (2001), The European Audiovisual Industry: An Overview, EIB Sector Paper, n.p.: European Investment Bank.

De Vany A. and W. D. Walls (1999), "Uncertainty in the Movie Industry: Does Star Power Reduce the Terror of the Box Office?" *Journal of Cultural Economics*, 23, pp. 285-318.

EAO (2006), *Focus 2006: World Film Market Trends*, European Audiovisual Observatory.

EAO (2005), *Press Release*, Eurofiction 2005: Total production of fiction in the largest 5 countries is on the up, 11 October.

EAO (2002), *Press Release*, The imbalance of trade in films and television programs between Europe and North America continues to deteriorate, 9 April.

European Union (2006), Interactive content and convergence: Implications for the information society, Final Report of a Study for the European Commission (DG Information Society and Media), By Screen Digest Ltd, CMS Hasche Sigle, Goldmedia Gmbh, Rightscom Ltd., October.

Financial Times (2006a), Paramount vs. Cruise: All down to the killer cut, 25 August, p. 13.

Financial Times (2006b), Hollywood's ultimatum: 'Show me the money, or else', Wall Street has applauded the tough tactics taken by Paramount against its former star, 26 August, p. 19.

Financial Times (2006c), MySpace sees link with leading search engine, 23 May, p. 17.

Financial Times (2006d), Google in bid to halt YouTube legal threat, 2 November, pp. 20; 27.

Financial Times (2007), Celluloid tsar strives to bend it for Britain, 8 June 2007, p. 13.

Fritz M. (2005), "Standardization Kick Starts Digital Cinema", *E-Content Magazine*, October.

Guillou, B. (2004), Online Distribution of Films, a study carried out for the European Audiovisual Observatory, May.

Hoskins, C., S. McFayden and A. Finn (1997), *Global Television and Film: An Introduction to the Economics of the Business*, Oxford: Clarendon Press.

Hughes, J. and K. Lang (2006), Transmutability: Digital Decontextualization, Manipulation, and Recontextualization as a New Source of Value in the Production and Consumption of Culture Products, *Proceedings of the 39th IEEE Hawaii International Conference on System Sciences*, pp. 1-10.

Husak, W. (2004), "Economic and Other Considerations for Digital Cinema, *Signal Processing: Image Communication* 19, pp. 921–936.

Image Communication (1993), Special Issue on Video Coding for 10 Mb/s" Signal Processing, February.

ITU-T (1995), Video Coding for Low Bitrate Communication", Recommendation H.263—Draft, Geneva, International Telecommunications Union, July.

Klaiessen, A. (2005), "Cable Leading Long-awaited Convergence of Internet and TV", *Advertising Age*, 76 (30) 25 July, p. 48.

Kodak Corporation (2002), Entertainment Imaging Position Paper.

Korris, J and M. Macedonia (2002), "The End of Celluloid: Digital Cinema Emerges", *Computer*, April, pp. 96-98.

Lampel, J. and J. Shamsie (2003), "Capabilities in Motion: New Organizational Forms and the Reshaping of the Hollywood Movie Industry", *Journal of Management Studies* 40 (8) December, pp. 2189-2210.

Lampel, J. and J. Shamsie (2003), Escalating Investment and Declining Returns: Red Queen Competition in the Motion Picture Industry, Evolution of Business Knowledge, EBK Working Paper 2005/26.

Lane, R. E. (1991), *The Market Experience*. Cambridge: Cambridge University Press.

Lange, A. (2005), "The Financial Situation of Television Companies in the European Union (1999-2004)", Strasbourg, European Audiovisual Observatory, September.

Langenderfer, J. and S. Kopp (2004), "The Digital Technology Revolution and Its Effect on the Market for Copyrighted Works: Is History Repeating Itself?" *Journal of Macromarketing,* 24 (1) June, pp. 17-30.

Le Gall, D. (1991), "MPEG: A Video Compression Standard for Multimedia Applications", *Communications of the ACM*, 34, April, pp. 46–58.

Liou, M. (1990), "Visual Telephony as an ISDN Application", *IEEE Communications Magazine*, 28, February, pp. 30–46.

McFadyen, S., C. Hoskins and A. Finn (1998), "The Effect of Cultural Differences on the International Co-production of Television Programs and Feature Films", *Canadian Journal of Communication*, 23 (4).

Mahadevan, B. (2000), "Business Models for Internet-Based E-Commerce: An Anatomy". *California Management Review*, Vol. 42, No. 4, Summer, pp. 55-69.

MPAA (2005a), *US Entertainment Industry: 2005 MPA Statistics*, Motion Picture Association of America.

MPAA (2005b), *2005 US Movie Attendance Study*, Motion Picture Association of America.

MPAA (2005c), *US Theatrical Market: 2005 Statistics*, Motion Picture Association of America.

MPAA (2006), *2006 Trade Barriers Report*, Motion Picture Association of America.

OECD (2004), *OECD Information Technology Outlook 2004*, Organisation for Economic Co-operation and Development, Paris.

OECD (2005a), "Digital Broadband Content: Scientific Publishing", DSTI/ICCP/IE(2004)11/FINAL, 2 September.

OECD (2005b), "Digital Broadband Content: Music", DSTI/ICCP/IE(2004)12/FINAL, 14 December.

OECD (2005c), "Digital Broadband Content: The Online Computer and Video Game Industry", DSTI/ICCP/IE(2004)13/FINAL, 12 May.

OECD (2005d), *Communications Outlook 2005*, Organisation for Economic Co-operation and Development, Paris.

OECD (2005e), "Report on Disclosure Issues related to the Use of Copy Control and Digital Rights Management Technologies", DSTI/CP(2005)15/FINAL.

OECD (2006a), *Information Technology Outlook 2006*, Organisation for Economic Co-operation and Development, Paris.

OECD (2006b), "Digital Broadband Content: Digital Content Strategies and Policies", DSTI/ICCP/IE(2005)3/FINAL, 19 May.

OECD (2006c), "Digital Broadband Content: Public Sector Information and Content", DSTI/ICCP/IE(2005)2/FINAL, 30 March.

OECD (2006d), OECD-BIAC Workshop on Future Online Audiovisual Services, Film and Video: Issues for Achieving Growth and Policy Objectives, at http://www.oecd.org/dataoecd/33/42/37866987.pdf

OECD (2007a), "The Economic Impact of Counterfeiting and Piracy, Results of Phase 1", pre-publication draft of the Phase I study report, www.oecd.org/sti/counterfeiting.

OECD (2007b), *OECD Communications Outlook 2007*, Organisation for Economic Co-operation and Development, Paris.

OECD (2007c), *Participative Web and User-Created Content: Web 2.0, Wikis and Social Networking*, Organisation for Economic Co-operation and Development, Paris.

Perry T. (2005), "The Sky is Falling", *IEEE Spectrum*, November.

Phillips, R. (2004)," The Global Export of Risk: Finance and the Film Business", *Competition & Change*, 8 (2), pp. 105-136.

Ravid, S. A. (1999), Information, Blockbusters, and Stars: A Study of the Film Industry, *Journal of Business*, 72 (4), pp. 463-492.

Reuters (2007), "BitTorrent, Joost Put Download Tech to Legal Use", 26 February, at EWeek.com

Ritson, M. (2006), "How To Add Venom to Film Promotion", *Marketing*, 9 August, p. 19.

Rogers, E. M. (1995), *Diffusion of Innovations*, Fourth Edition. New York: Free Press.

Scott, A. (2002), "A New Map of Hollywood: The Production and Distribution of American Motion Pictures", *Regional Studies,* 36 (9), pp. 957–975.

Screen Digest (2005), Press release: Online DVD rentals (DVD by post) are set to revolutionize the video rental market, 15 November.

Sears, G., W. Murray and D. Drisdell (2006), "Status of Digital Production in Canada", report prepared for the Department of Canadian Heritage, by the Kelly-Sears Consulting Group, 11 April.

Shanklin, W. (2002), "What Businesses Can Learn from the Movies", *Business Horizons*, January-February, pp. 23-28.

Silver, J. and F. Alpert (2003), "Digital Dawn: A Revolution in Movie Distribution?" *Business Horizons*, September-October, pp. 57-66.

Simpson, N. (2004), "Coming Attractions: A Comparative History of the Hollywood Studio System and the Porn Business, *Historical Journal of Film, Radio and Television,* 24 (4), pp. 635-652.

Stabell, C. B. and Ø. D. Fjeldstad (1998), "Configuring Value for Competitive Advantage: On Chains, Shops and Networks", *Strategic Management Journal* 19 (5), pp. 413-437.

UK Department for Culture, Media and Sport (2002), *Screen Digest Report on the implications of Digital Technology on the Film Industry*, September.

UK Department of Culture, Media and Sport (1998), *Creative Industries – Mapping document – Section 0.7, Film*, London.

UNESCO (2005), Survey on National Cinematography, UNESCO Cultural Industries and Enterprises, Paris.

US Bureau of Labor Statistics (2005), May 2005 National Industry-Specific Occupational Employment and Wage Estimates, NAICS 512100 - Motion Picture and Video Industries.

US Business Census (2002), *Motion Picture and Video Industries*, Washington: US Census Bureau, Industry Series, November 2004.

Vogel H. (2006), *Entertainment Industry Economics – A Guide for Financial Analysis* (5th Edition), Cambridge University Press, Cambridge.

Vogel, H. and E. Christiansen (2006), "Enhancing the Role of SMEs in Global Value Chains: Preliminary Analysis of the Cinema Industry", paper for the Working Party on SMEs and Entrepreneurship, Centre for Entrepreneurship, SMEs and Local Development, OECD, Paris, 6-7 June.

Zerdick A., A. Picot, K. Schrape, A. Artopé, K. Goldhammer, U. Lange, E. Vierkant, E. López-Escobar and R. Silverstone (2000), *E-conomics: Strategies for the Digital Marketplace*, European Communication Council Report, Springer-Verlag, Berlin.

Zhu, K. (2001), "Internet-based Distribution of Digital Videos: The Economic Impacts of Digitisation on the Motion Picture Industry", *Electronic Markets*, 11 (4), pp. 273-280.

Online references cited and consulted

(OR1) Intel, revelations unlock door to the digital home, www.intel.com/pressroom/archive/releases/20050118corp.htm

(OR2) Call for European cinema to unite, Michael Osborn http://news.bbc.co.uk/1/hi/entertainment/film/4124706.stm

(OR3) Online movies given release boost, http://news.bbc.co.uk/1/hi/entertainment/4871392.stm

(OR4) Movielink Launches First U.S. electronic download-to-own service for major motion pictures, marking important milestone in digital distribution of movies, Business Wire, April 3, 2006, http://www.findarticles.com/p/articles/mim0EIN/is2006April3/ain16116082

(OR5) www.cinemanow.com

(OR6) Sony and GUBA pioneer online movie distribution deal, July 14, 2006, http://www.techsmec.com/2006/07/14/sony-and-guba-pioneer-online-movie-distribution-deal/

(OR7) iTunes' movie downloads the 'tipping point' for online movie distribution?, Michael Greeson, CEO, Co-Founder of The Diffusion Group, TDG Research, June 22, 2006, http://news.digitaltrends.com/talkback128.html

(OR8) www.sightsound.com

(OR9) Atopia announces new web-based film distribution initiatives, February 21, 2006, http://www.atopia.com/pr.e/7034.php

(OR10) Warner Bros. to sell movies and TV shows on Internet, Julie Bosman and Tom Zeller Jr., May 9, 2006, http://www.nytimes.com/2006/05/09/business/media/09movie.html

(OR11) www.brightcove.com

(OR12) Google, Yahoo testing cable TV model online -- Where will it lead?, Carl Howe, August 3, 2006, http://Internet.seekingalpha.com/article/14926

(OR13) Apple, Netflix, Amazon, Comcast or Microsoft: who's the digital movie winner?, David Jackson, August 3, 2006, http://media.seekingalpha.com/article/14925

(OR14) Comcast buys Net video delivery provider, Stefanie Olsen, CNETNews.com, June 28, 2006, http://news.zdnet.com/2100-9588_22-6089131.html

(OR15) 'Bollywood' produces real-life drama,
http://abcnews.go.com/International/story?id=81141&page=1

(OR16) Eros, Intel align to launch 'B On Demand', world's largest official on–demand 'Bollywood' portal using Intel® Viiv™ Technology
http://www.intel.com/pressroom/archive/releases/20060105corp_k.htm

(OR17) What is "Bollywood"?
http://www.bollywoodworld.com/whatisbollywood/index.htm

(OR18) Indian film in Internet distribution wave
http://www.hinduonnet.com/thehindu/2003/12/11/stories/2003121104582200.htm

Appendix A

NORTH AMERICAN STATISTICAL DEFINITION OF THE MOTION PICTURE SECTOR

PART 1. 2002 NAICS

5121 MOTION PICTURE AND VIDEO INDUSTRIES

This industry group comprises establishments primarily engaged in the production and/or distribution of motion pictures, videos, television programs, or commercials; in the exhibition of motion pictures; or in the provision of postproduction and related services.

51211 MOTION PICTURE AND VIDEO PRODUCTION

This industry comprises establishments primarily engaged in producing, or producing and distributing motion pictures, videos, television programs, or television commercials.

512110 MOTION PICTURE AND VIDEO PRODUCTION

This industry comprises establishments primarily engaged in producing, or producing and distributing motion pictures, videos, television programs, or television commercials.

51212 MOTION PICTURE AND VIDEO DISTRIBUTION

This industry comprises establishments primarily engaged in acquiring distribution rights and distributing film and video productions to motion picture theaters, television networks and stations, and exhibitors.

512120 MOTION PICTURE AND VIDEO DISTRIBUTION

This industry comprises establishments primarily engaged in acquiring distribution rights and distributing film and video productions to motion picture theaters, television networks and stations, and exhibitors.

51213 MOTION PICTURE AND VIDEO EXHIBITION

This industry comprises establishments primarily engaged in operating motion pictur theatres and/or exhibiting motion pictures or videos at film festivals, and so forth.

512131 MOTION PICTURE THEATERS (EXCEPT DRIVE-INS)

This industry comprises establishments primarily engaged in operating motion pictur theatres (except drive-ins) and/or exhibiting motion pictures or videos at film festivals and so forth.

512132 DRIVE-IN MOTION PICTURE THEATERS

This industry comprises establishments primarily engaged in operating drive-in motio picture theatres.

51219 POSTPRODUCTION SERVICES AND OTHER MOTION PICTURE AN VIDEO INDUSTRIES

This industry comprises establishments primarily engaged in providing postproductio services and other services to the motion picture industry, including specialized motio picture or video postproduction services, such as editing, film/tape transfers, subtitling credits, closed captioning, and computer-produced graphics, animation and special effects as well as developing and processing motion picture film.

512191 TELEPRODUCTION AND OTHER POSTPRODUCTION SERVICES

This industry comprises establishments primarily engaged in providing specialize motion picture or video postproduction services, such as editing, film/tape transfers subtitling, credits, closed captioning, and animation and special effects.

512199 OTHER MOTION PICTURE AND VIDEO INDUSTRIES

This industry comprises establishments primarily engaged in providing motion pictur and video services (except motion picture and video production, distribution, exhibitior and teleproduction and other postproduction services).

Appendix B

THE INDIAN MOTION PICTURE INDUSTRY

"Bollywood" is certainly the best known segment of the Indian film industry, but this term refers only to the Mumbai-based Hindi-language film industry. This represents about a third of total film production in India, the rest of the industry being in other language groups (mainly Punjabi, Tamil, Telugu, Bengali, Malayalam and Kannada). Bollywood films are usually musicals. Few are made without at least one song-and-dance number. Indian audiences expect each film to contain all of the same elements – music and dance, love interest, comedy and action. Such productions are called "masala movies", after the potent spice mixture.

Financial and industry structure

Bollywood budgets are usually modest by Hollywood standards. Sets, costumes, special effects and cinematography were less than world-class until the mid-to-late 1990s. But as western films and television programs gained wider distribution, there was increasing pressure for Bollywood films to attain the same production levels. Sequences shot overseas have proven popular, so Mumbai film crews are increasingly peripatetic, filming in Australia, New Zealand, the United Kingdom, continental Europe and elsewhere.

Indian producers are drawing in more funding for big-budget films shot within India. Funding for Bollywood films comes often from private distributors and a few large studios. Indian banks were once forbidden to lend money to film productions, but this ban has been lifted recently. In general, finances are not regulated to the degree that all of the sources of investment are transparent.

The industry is very loosely structured. Although the studios co-ordinate distribution, much as in other countries, virtually all Indian films are independent productions to the extent that each production typically results from a one-time collaboration between freelance contractors.

Although imported films have a small share of the cinema market, imports do penetrate this market via television and satellite. On the other hand, Indian films now earn export revenues, mostly from cinemas in the United Kingdom, Canada and the US, increasingly from a non-Indian audience who see Bollywood as an emerging film genre. Moreover, as more Indians migrate to these countries, they form a growing market for upscale Indian films. US studios such as Warner Bros. and Twentieth Century Fox are acquiring business interests in India.

Online distribution

Overall Internet penetration figures are low relative to India's total population, but at the end of 2005 there were 7 million Internet subscribers and 60 million users, of which 885 000 were subscribers to high-speed broadband, these subscriptions increasing by around 50% in the last quarter of 2005 alone. Indian film producers are very proactive in digital distribution. In December 2003, the Hindi film *Supari* became the world's first feature film to go on first release as an Internet download (using Kaza peer-to-peer technology). Take-up was very modest – just over 200 downloads in the first three weeks at a cost of USD 2.99 – but the experiment showed the awareness of Indian producers that electronic distribution will have a major part to play in the development of their industry. The technology offers efficiencies in film markets such as India where production values typically are low by world standards but domestic audiences are extremely large.

In the period since *Supari* many more Indian films have been distributed online. Eros International, the single largest international distributor in the Indian film industry, has teamed up with Intel Corporation to provide on-demand online video delivery services via Intel® Viiv™ PC technology. Intel's collaboration with Eros International will enable the company to deliver its premium content library over broadband Internet to more than 50 million South Asian consumers plus millions of other consumers.

Digital cinema

Bollywood seems to be set to embrace the new digital cinema technology. Several local distribution companies are converting about 1 000 screens throughout the country and in the next three to four years it is expected that close to 4 000 cinemas will be converted to digital screening at an estimated cost of USD 2 billion. Hughes India (a subsidiary of the US Hughes Network Systems) has teamed up with Valuegroup, a domestic film company, to roll out digital screening in a further 2 000 cinemas over the next four years. Hughes Network has set up a satellite-based digital film hub in Gurgaon near Delhi.

Digital cinema is seen to have the ability to penetrate smaller rural communities more cost effectively. At present new films are released only in larger cities because of the costs of producing enough celluloid prints for wider distribution. Although India has a population of over 1 billion, there are only about 12 000 film exhibition sites and it is not practical to release a new film at more than about 200 sites at any one time.

Cheaper modes of digitisation are being employed that involve generally low-quality projection equipment. Both cinema owners and consumers in smaller Indian cities are willing to compromise on quality in return for access to the latest releases. However, should this pragmatism lead to adoption of different production and exhibition standards, it is likely the industry will encounter significant co-ordination costs later on. But despite or perhaps because of the lack of technology co-ordination, digital rollout in India has started attracting global interest. For example, the French firm Thomson has a joint venture with VSNL, an Indian telecom company, to offer end-to-end solutions for digital cinema. This will include distribution of films via satellite as well as digital rights management. Likewise, Sony Pictures Entertainment is at the preliminary stages of entering the digital cinema industry in India.

The information upon which this profile was constructed was derived from OR 15, 16, 17 and 18 (see bibliography), supplemented with information from interviews with individuals active in the Mumbai film industry.

OECD PUBLICATIONS, 2, rue André-Pascal, 75775 PARIS CEDEX 16
PRINTED IN FRANCE
(93 2008 01 1 P) ISBN 978-92-64-04329-9 – No. 56011 2008

CPSIA information can be obtained at www.ICGtesting.com
Printed in the USA
LVOW12s0947100114

368788LV00003B/46/P

9 789264 043299